THE BLACK WOMAN'S GUIDE TO OVERCOMING DOMESTIC VIOLENCE

tools to
move beyond trauma,
reclaim freedom &
create the life you deserve

SHAVONNE J. MOORE-LOBBAN, PhD
& ROBYN L. GOBIN, PhD

New Harbinger Publications, Inc.

NEW HARBINGER PUBLICATIONS is a registered trademark of New Harbinger Publications, Inc.

New Harbinger Publications is an employee-owned company.

Lucille Clifton, "won't you celebrate with me" from *The Book of Light*. Copyright © 1993 by Lucille Clifton. Reprinted with the permission of The Permissions Company, LLC on behalf of Copper Canyon Press, coppercanyonpress.org.

Distributed in Canada by Raincoast Books

Copyright © 2022 by Shavonne J. Moore-Lobban and Robyn L. Gobin
New Harbinger Publications, Inc.
5674 Shattuck Avenue
Oakland, CA 94609
www.newharbinger.com

Cover design by Amy Daniel; Acquired by Georgia Kolias; Edited by Teja Watson

MIX
Paper from responsible sources
FSC
www.fsc.org   FSC® C011935

Library of Congress Cataloging-in-Publication Data

Names: Moore-Lobban, Shavonne J., author. | Gobin, Robyn L., author.
Title: The Black woman's guide to overcoming domestic violence : tools to move beyond trauma, reclaim freedom, and create the life you deserve / Shavonne J. Moore-Lobban, PhD, Robyn L. Gobin, PhD.
Description: Oakland, CA : New Harbinger Publications, [2022] | Includes bibliographical references.
Identifiers: LCCN 2021062160 | ISBN 9781684039340 (trade paperback)
Subjects: LCSH: Intimate partner violence. | Family violence. | Women, Black--Violence against. | Women, Black--Abuse of. | BISAC: FAMILY & RELATIONSHIPS / Abuse / Domestic Partner Abuse | SELF-HELP / Abuse
Classification: LCC HV6626 .M669 2022 | DDC 362.82/92082--dc23/eng/20220126
LC record available at https://lccn.loc.gov/2021062160

Printed in the United States of America

24	23	22							
10	9	8	7	6	5	4	3	2	1

First Printing

To our husbands, who support our dreams and
encourage us to achieve them.

To our family, who have always grounded us in
and surrounded us with love.

For the beautiful Black women of the world,
who are survivors in every regard:

We honor your strength, courage, wisdom, and vulnerability.

Contents

Foreword

Who will sing an upbeat song for Black women?

We will sing it for ourselves and the world will marvel at how long we hold our notes.

—Thema Bryant, PhD

In a world in which we as Black women are bombarded with downbeats, stereotypes, stigma, exclusion, and violations, we have the capacity to not only heal but to write a new, upbeat song with our lives. While domestic violence has many effects, it does not have the final say on who you are and who you can be. Whether the abuse you experienced was psychological, physical, economic, sexual, spiritual, or all of the above, I hope a part of you will start to believe you deserve so much better.

Welcome to your new chapter, your new beginning. I am overjoyed that as a survivor (or the supporter of a survivor) you picked up this book. You made it despite the put-downs, mistreatment, disrespect, and disappointment. This book, written by two brilliant and compassionate Black women healers and scholars, provides a road map to reclaiming and rebuilding your life. Abusive relationships often take so much from you, including self-confidence, mental health, physical health, and time. As you work toward your restoration, I want you to know that the most important component you will reclaim is yourself. For some of you who experienced early trauma, this may mean claiming yourself for the first time.

This moment is a gift and an investment in yourself. It requires actively pushing back on the ways your former partner(s) made you feel and think about yourself. You get to write a new anthem, and when you start to feel heavy with self-doubt, this resource will serve as a constant reminder that you are worthy. You are worthy of love, respect, and peace of mind.

As Black women we have often been raised to be super strong, to endure, and to persevere no matter what. This pressure to be strong for everyone else while neglecting our needs is a setup for abuse and a form of dehumanization. In this season of your life, may you get in touch with your humanity, which includes having breathing room, permission to feel all of your feelings, and space to heal as you remember the truth of your identity. This book provides a blueprint for your recovery that attends to all of your beautiful layers—spiritual, cultural, psychological, physical, and social.

The final chapter is for those who will support you on the journey. The African proverb says "It takes a village to raise a child." I would offer that it takes a village to heal a woman. As you are reading this empowering book, I hope you will give yourself permission to break out of isolation and distrust. Connection with community is an important aspect of healing, so whether you reach out to a psychologist, pastor, friend, or online support group, remember that you do not have to walk this journey alone.

As you begin this book, I want to encourage you to make a personal commitment to complete it. Sometimes motivation for the healing journey can fade. However long it takes you to process, reflect, digest, and apply it, there is something for you in each chapter.

Finally, I want to intentionally and directly push back against the stigma that Black women who are abused are weak or stupid. Those are lies. To survive everything that you did took strength and wisdom, which may have often been unrecognized, perhaps even by you.

You showed up in the relationship space with hope and love. Those are beautiful qualities, and they are essential qualities for healthy relationships. I share this because it is important for the unhealthy relationship(s) of yesterday to not permanently harden you to the possibility that there are caring people in the world—and yes, potentially in your future.

So wherever and however you find yourself in this moment on the healing path—weeping, angry, afraid, or numb—know that we see you and care about your recovery. There are incredible Black women, famous and unknown, ancestors and those living in this season, who are also survivors. They comprise the great cloud of witnesses that are cheering for your rebirth. Turn the page and let the journey begin.

—Thema Bryant, PhD
Pepperdine University
Coauthor of *The Antiracism Handbook:*
Practical Tools to Shift Your Mindset and
Uproot Racism in Your Life and Community

Preface

We feel honored to bring you this book.

We thank you for trusting us to journey along with you, and we pray that this book is a resource that provides you with the information, encouragement, and support that you may need.

As you move through your journey to healing and wholeness, we hope that this book reminds you that you are not alone; that what happened to you is not your fault; and that you have the power to transform any feelings of brokenness that you experience.

We believe in your strength, power, and resilience. We also encourage your vulnerability, as you open your heart and mind to the healing process.

—Dr. Shavonne J. Moore-Lobban
and Dr. Robyn L. Gobin

Your Journey to Healing and Wholeness

As a Black woman and a survivor of domestic violence, you deserve joy, peace, pleasure, and fulfillment in your life—and healing is the gateway to these things. But you should know that healing doesn't happen on its own. It requires intention, effort, and dedication. We believe in your ability to heal, and we hope the words of this book will help you to realize just how powerful and capable you are of thriving—despite the challenges you have faced.

This book is written by Black women, for Black women. Both of us are Black women who were raised by Black women, and who continue to be surrounded and supported by the knowledge, love, and wisdom of Black women. We take pride in our identity and approached this book with that pride in mind. We both grew up in the church and identify with the spiritual understanding of grace, compassion, and healing. We bring those perspectives to this book, and we invite you to bring them to yourself as well. We hope you can approach this book with grace and compassion for yourself, as well as a belief that healing is possible.

We both feel connected to a larger purpose in this world, part of which involves supporting Black women in their journey to heal from trauma. As licensed psychologists, we have spent our professional careers doing this work. Trained in understanding and treating trauma, we work from a womanist, culturally aware, and social justice–driven framework to center and promote Black women's health and wellness. We are experienced in working with diverse groups of people, and we very much enjoy this work. We are also passionate about uplifting Black women, specifically. Our collective experiences and desire for hope and healing have brought us to a place of coauthoring this book, which we hope will be especially helpful for you.

This book is meant to be a collaborative process of us journeying along with you. We will bring our knowledge, experience, and background to this book, and you, naturally, will do the same. We have written this book with language that speaks directly to you. We will often provide examples, to help support your understanding of the material. Some examples may feel specific and relevant to you; some may not. It is okay for your experience to differ because every survivor is different. You are the expert on your life, and you know what connects with your experiences. We honor your right to choose. We encourage you to take what is helpful and use it to move forward in your healing journey.

The language of this book is written for you, as someone who has "survived" domestic violence. We also acknowledge that "surviving" is a process and a journey. You may have survived, and you may also be surviving. You may or may not identify with the label "survivor." That label is meant to convey our understanding that you have made it out of a scary, harmful, and dangerous time in your life. But as we mentioned, we also acknowledge that you may still be in the process of making it out. Perhaps you have left or perhaps you are still leaving. Wherever you are within your journey, we welcome you. If you are still finding your way out, we encourage your safety in using this book. Consider keeping it in a location that an abusive partner does not access, such as at your job, at a friend or family member's house, under your car seat (if you have your own car), or in another private location.

Domestic violence impacts women from all ethnic backgrounds, but as a Black woman you are particularly vulnerable to it. We intentionally center and honor your experience as a Black woman. We believe that our identity as Black women influences our experiences in the world and with other people. It also influences our expectations and understandings of ourselves. We will explore the cultural influences that surround domestic violence, to promote your healing through a culturally informed perspective. We hope that you explore your identity as a means of engaging your power, connecting with yourself, and, ultimately, thriving after your trauma.

We are deeply committed to Black women's health and wholeness. Our intention for this book is to help you heal from domestic violence in a solution-focused and practical way. We offer healing solutions that are research-based and theory-informed. The healing strategies we provide are based on the best research available and center on six core themes: *safety, trust, self-esteem, guilt and shame, power and control,* and *intimacy.* We chose to focus on these themes because they are the areas most disrupted by domestic violence, and we have developed expertise in addressing them in our therapeutic work with Black women survivors. The skills and healing strategies are offered in the spirit of love, admiration, and respect for you, as a Black woman.

In chapters 1–3, we begin by providing foundational knowledge and information, to help you better understand the context and multifaceted impact of domestic violence, the factors that make Black women's experience with domestic violence different, and the oppressive factors that keep Black women in abusive situations.

Next, in chapters 4–9, we provide tools to help you explore how domestic violence has uniquely impacted you, and to practice skills and solutions to help you progress toward internal healing and freedom. In these chapters, to demonstrate key concepts, we share the stories of women we have had the honor to walk alongside on their healing journeys. Names and details have been changed to protect privacy and safety.

Finally, in chapters 10–11, we provide guidance for enriching your healing journey with self-care and by seeking support from others. In doing so, we provide practical strategies for how friends, family members, non-abusive partners, clergy, and health care professionals can best support your healing.

Woven into each chapter are open-ended questions meant to stimulate reflection and self-discovery. We invite you to keep a designated healing journal nearby while reading this book, and to write down your responses to the questions in each chapter. Journaling will help you get the most out of the healing strategies and tools in the book, by applying the information to your own life. It may be tempting to skip over the questions, but we believe they are integral to your healing. The healing journey has ups and downs, and it is different for each person. The healing skills and strategies we provide will work best for you if you take the time to see how they fit your personal needs, background, goals, and experiences. Reading this book alone is good, but using a journal to pause, reflect, and respond to the prompts helps you receive the most benefit.

We hope you will draw on your strength, resilience, and vulnerability as you progress on this healing journey. To support you in this, we open each chapter with poetry and quotes from Black women. We believe there is power in words, especially the words of Black women. Poetry is healing and can provide the balm needed to soothe your soul and help you keep going when you feel like giving up. Poetry reminds you that you are not alone. It is a powerful way to connect to ancestors and other Black women who have overcome and survived unimaginable pain and trauma. We hope the poems and quotes included in this book enrich your healing journey.

Beginning the healing journey can create a mix of emotions: fear, optimism, excitement, and hesitancy. No matter how you are feeling, we want to acknowledge that your feelings are valid. Because we know how strong emotions can be, we want to equip you with two tools up front that you can lean on throughout your healing journey: grounding and journaling. We have already reviewed the benefits of journaling. While reading this book, whenever you see a prompt, you are encouraged to pause, reflect, and respond in your designated healing journal.

Grounding is a skill that you can use to connect with your body in moments when you are feeling emotionally overwhelmed. On the healing journey, even when there is no immediate threat or danger, you might feel unsafe, especially when remembering some specific domestic violence events. Grounding helps you calm down, assess your present environment, and remember that you are safe, even when your thoughts, memories, or body take you back to the abuse you experienced.

To ground yourself, you may want to touch something physically present in the room—this helps you come back to the present moment.

For example, you can ground yourself by feeling the weight of this book in your hands, gently pressing your feet against the floor beneath you, or feeling the weight of your body sitting on your chair or lying on your bed. We encourage you to try any of these grounding techniques whenever you feel uneasy or overwhelmed while reading this book.

Healing takes time. It can be tempting to want to rush the healing process, but we encourage you to focus more on growing along the healing journey, rather than reaching a destination or outcome. For many, healing can be a lifelong journey. Honor yourself by giving your mind, body, and spirit the time needed to fully heal and be free. Be present for the journey and know that we are rooting for you. Black women are often capable of more than we give ourselves credit for. We believe in you. You got this!

CHAPTER 1

Understanding Domestic Violence

There's power in allowing yourself to be known and heard in owning your unique story, in using your authentic voice. And there's grace in being willing to know and hear others. This, for me, is how we become.

—Michelle Obama

Assayiah was with her partner, James, for four years. The beginning years were exciting, full of date nights, romantic gestures, and time getting to know each other's family and friends. Everyone liked James, but a few of her friends and family members thought he could be jealous and possessive. Eventually, everyone decided it was just "young love" and supported their relationship.

At some point, before Assayiah realized it, she was not spending as much time with her friends and family. Assayiah and James began their own family and had their first child. Assayiah wanted to stay close to her family so they could help with the baby, but James thought they should be more "independent" and on their own. He surprised her by putting a down payment on a home that was an hour away from her family, which made it difficult for them to visit.

James also decided that Assayiah should stay home with their child and not return to work after maternity leave. Assayiah was conflicted, because she loved her career. James insisted that staying home was the "motherly" thing to do. He began giving her money for daily expenses. Over time, he showed himself to be more controlling.

James often insulted her parenting, her appearance, and her ability to "take care of the home." He was verbally abusive toward her, called her names, and started giving her less money.

Assayiah felt like she had no one to turn to. This was not the life she imagined for herself. This was not the life they began with. They shared a child; she was worried she would lose custody if she left. She wanted to have a family for her child, but she worried about the type of family environment they would have if she stayed in the abusive relationship.

Assayiah was finally ready to talk with her family about it, but right before she was going to see them, James physically assaulted her. He punched her multiple times and threw her into the bedroom wall. She was afraid to see her family with visible bruises, unsure whether they would understand how things were behind closed doors. She knew her family suspected things were not going well for *her at home, but she also experienced them as being silent and not stepping in to help. They didn't understand why someone as "smart and beautiful" as her wouldn't just change a situation that wasn't working for her.*

There are many relationships like Assayiah's and James's. If you feel any connections to her story, you are not alone.

Before you read further, take a moment to think about your response to Assayiah's story. Grab your journal and write down how you feel. What emotions came up as you read about her experience and thought about your own? Can you relate to her story? Are parts of her experience familiar to you?

As you saw in Assayiah's story, her family and friends did not fully understand the abuse within her relationship. Assayiah herself did not always understand it. Misunderstandings are common, because violence and abuse in relationships are not always talked about.

In this chapter, you will come to understand this violence and abuse as experiences known as *domestic violence.* You will also read about some common myths and facts about domestic violence, which are important to keep in mind as you process and consider your own experiences. And you will explore the things that contribute to silence and shaming, and that impact your mental and physical well-being as a Black woman survivor of domestic violence.

What Is Domestic Violence?

You may have heard different terms used to describe violence and abuse in relationships. Perhaps you have heard the terms *domestic violence, domestic abuse, intimate partner violence, intimate partner abuse, violence against women, spousal abuse, partner abuse,* and others.

There is no perfect label to describe the atrocities that one endures in an abusive relationship. In some ways, the word "domestic" seems to imply that partners are living with each other, or that there is a domestic nature to the relationship. "Intimate" may be misleading, assuming sexual (or other) intimacy exists in the relationship, which may not be the case. Other terms like "partner" and "spouse" indicate an established and committed relationship, but the abusive partner may not be thought of as a partner at all. They could be a boyfriend, girlfriend, person you were dating, or even someone who you hooked up with.

For consistency, and in keeping with the most used term, we will use the term *domestic violence* as an umbrella term to encompass all aspects of these definitions. *Domestic violence* is purposeful intimidation, physical assault, sexual assault, battery, or other abusive acts that someone commits against you. We will also use the term "partner" in relation to all types of partners listed above, and with respect for gender neutrality.

Myths and Facts

Domestic violence is not always understood. What is true or untrue about it can be confusing, which certainly makes it hard to change. Within your own process of understanding the relationship, and deciding on the steps to leave it, perhaps you were unclear about what was happening and why it was happening. The misconceptions about abusive relationships can be present within friends and family as well. You see this in Assayiah's story, as she and her family tried to understand James's controlling behavior.

So, it's important for us to clarify some of the common myths and facts about domestic violence. As you read them, take note of which ones might be old or new information for you.

MYTH: *Violence and abuse in relationships is always physical.*

FACT: *Domestic violence can include physical violence, but it is not limited to physical violence.*

Physical violence is one, but not the only, form of domestic violence. Others forms of abuse—such as sexual violence, psychological or emotional abuse, financial abuse, and stalking—are also considered domestic violence. You saw examples of psychological and financial abuse in Assayiah's experience.

Let's explore each type of abuse.

Physical Violence: Physical violence and abuse is where an abusive partner uses physical force, such as hitting, kicking, biting, punching, slapping, smacking, or more. They might also use weapons, which is considered a severe form of physical violence.

Sexual Violence: Sexual violence and abuse is where an abusive partner forces you to engage in sexual acts that you do not want to engage in. It can include unwanted sexual contact, such as kissing, touching, oral sex, penetration, or more. Although domestic violence is commonly associated with physical violence, many women also report sexual violence in the relationship. Some of the surveys that explore sexual violence in relationships also explore control of reproductive or sexual health as a type of sexual abuse. Examples include partners refusing to wear a condom, pretending to take birth control, or otherwise manipulating the chances of reproduction against your will.

There is also a myth that people cannot be sexually assaulted within a romantic relationship. Have you ever heard that? The truth is that being in a relationship does not automatically mean consent for sexual activity. Being in a relationship is not a free pass for on-demand sexual experiences. Every sexual experience should be consented to by both people in the relationship. Importantly, you have the right to withdraw your consent at any time. In other words, saying yes to a particular encounter does not mean that you have said yes to all encounters.

Psychological or Emotional Abuse: Psychological abuse is where an abusive partner expresses their aggression through screaming, name-calling, insulting, belittling, or humiliation. The goal of this behavior is to gain more control in the relationship.

Stalking: Stalking is where an abusive person shows a pattern of harassing and threatening behavior, in a manner that might make you fear for your safety. Stalking can occur in person: for example, showing up to your home, work, or other known locations. However, as technology has increased, virtual stalking has also become more problematic. For example, an abusive partner may monitor your online/social media profiles or activity. They might also track your location using your phone's GPS. Thankfully, smartphones and social media platforms have improved their options of allowing you to turn off your phone's locator ability, or to stop social media posts from automatically tagging your location.

Financial and Economic Abuses: Financial and economic abuse is where an abusive partner exhibits control over your access to finances, in a way that creates financial dependence on them. Examples include limiting access to mutual finances (a joint bank account, for example), stopping you from working, sabotaging your employment, withholding shared assets, controlling how you spend money, mismanaging money you share, or even creating large shared debt in your name.

MYTH: *This is only happening to "me." "I" am alone.*

FACT: *You are not alone.*

Although you may have felt alone in your experience, unfortunately domestic violence happens around the world. When the World Health Organization (WHO 2005) conducted a survey of women's health and domestic violence from women in multiple countries, they found that domestic violence was widespread around the world, and that most countries reported that at least a quarter of people experienced domestic violence.

Within the US specifically, millions of people experience domestic violence in their lifetime. According to the National Intimate Partner and Sexual Violence Survey (NISVS), one in three women, or approximately 43.6 million women, experience domestic violence. Although you may feel alone in experiencing such unexpected and hurtful behavior from your partner, the difficult truth is that domestic violence is widespread (D'Inverno et al. 2019).

It's important to know that as a Black woman, you are particularly vulnerable to domestic violence. Another NISVS survey showed that roughly four out of every ten Black women, and one out of every two multiracial women, experience multiple forms of abuse from their partner during their lifetime (Black et al. 2011). The CDC's National Center for Injury Prevention and Control also reports that Black women experience physical violence, sexual violence, stalking, and psychological aggression by an abusive partner more often than White, Hispanic, or Asian women (Niolon et al. 2017). Additionally, within the Black community, rates of severe physical domestic violence may be higher for women who identify as African American than for those who identify as Caribbean (Lacey et al. 2016).

With this being said, an important consideration to hold is that all these numbers represent individuals who disclosed their abuse. There may be higher numbers when you consider those who have not disclosed or who were not surveyed. You will read more about the reasons and factors that go into staying silent later on, in chapter 7, when we discuss shame and guilt. For now, the takeaway message is that you are not alone: this is a global problem that impacts many women. And the numbers, though high, still may not represent the true number of people who experience such victimization.

MYTH: *This is "my" fault.*

FACT: *Domestic violence is not your fault.*

Being abused is never your fault. There is nothing you did wrong and nothing you could have done right. You were not "asking" for it to happen. Ultimately, you are not to blame for someone else's behavior toward you, even if your abusive partner tried to manipulate you into thinking that you are.

You might have heard statements from friends and family such as "Why did you provoke them?" or "Haven't you learned what sets them off?" These statements are known as *victim blaming.* Victim blaming is just what it sounds like: blaming you for behavior that should be blamed on the person who is abusing you. The fact is that abusive partners are responsible for their own actions. The ownership of the abusive behavior should lie with the abuser.

MYTH: *You can just leave an abusive relationship.*

FACT: *Abusive partners make it a point to create situations that are extremely difficult for you to get out of.*

You may have heard people say that you should simply leave the relationship and stop "allowing" such treatment. We see this in Assayiah's situation. Her friends and family did not understand how someone like her could be in an abusive relationship. Statements such as "Why don't you just leave?" may stem from well-intended but misguided information. Remember, you did not allow yourself to be abused. Again, those statements are victim-blaming, and we know they can leave you feeling alone, silenced, unseen, unprotected, and cast aside. You should not have to feel that way.

Those statements are made without awareness of the complexities of abusive situations. For example, Assayiah was isolated from her family, which made it hard for the people who cared about her to truly notice what was going on with her. Perhaps you can relate to that experience; perhaps your friends and family had little to no access to you when you needed their help. With little understanding of your reality, friends and family may think leaving is simple, but the truth is, there's nothing simple about it.

MYTH: *Men are always abusers and women are always victims.*

FACT: *Domestic violence is not always between men and women, and even when it is, women can be abusers.*

There are high rates of domestic violence within same-sex relationships. In fact, one researcher found that almost 50 percent of lesbians experience domestic violence in their lifetime. They also found that psychological and emotional abuse were the most common forms of domestic violence in those relationships (Badenes-Ribera et al. 2015). One researcher reviewed four decades' worth of data and information, to better understand domestic violence within same-sex and opposite-sex relationships, and among people of color specifically. They found that people of color in same-sex relationships reported higher rates of domestic violence than individuals in opposite-sex relationships (West 2012). This highlights the fact that domestic violence is not limited to one gender or type of relationship.

Although women are abused more often than men are, women can also be abusive: they can abuse other women and they can also abuse men. When it comes to physical violence, reports have shown that both partners can engage in some form of physical aggression, ranging from minor to major acts. Women tend to engage in minor aggressive behaviors, such as making threats, throwing objects, or slapping their partner, while men tend to engage in more severe violence, such as choking (West 2012). The NISVS found that about four out of every ten Black men, and four out of every ten multiracial men, experienced domestic violence during their lifetime (Black et al. 2011). These numbers represent both situations where men abused other men, and situations where women abused men.

MYTH: *Violence and abuse within relationships is an adult problem.*

FACT: *Violence and abuse happens within youth relationships as well.*

Youth relationships are not exempt from domestic violence. If you first experienced violence in a teen relationship and later experienced adult domestic violence, know that this is not uncommon. The term most used to describe this type of domestic violence is *teen dating violence.* According to the NISVS, sixteen million adults who experienced intimate partner violence also experienced dating violence before the age of eighteen (Smith et al. 2018).

Why Does Domestic Violence Occur?

Domestic violence is primarily understood as being about 1) gender-role stereotypes and 2) power and control. We can see both when we look at the ways women have historically been treated as subservient to men, and how men have historically been encouraged to show power and control over women.

Gender-Role Stereotypes

Throughout time, women have been viewed as the property of someone else. For centuries, their place in society was supposed to be quiet and reserved, and their experiences were largely ignored. During slavery, Black women were thought of as the property of the White men who owned them. In addition to forced outdoor labor, Black women were also made to clean the home, cook the meals, raise the children (theirs and others'), be wet nurses, and generally serve the White family. They were expected to do these things without complaining or expecting anything in return. In fact, complaining or expecting anything in return could result in violence and harm.

Many Black women were also sexually abused by White men and were unable to speak out about it. You may have heard that sexual abuse cannot happen within a relationship, a myth that is connected to the idea that women belong to the person they are in a relationship with—in the same way that Black women were the property of White men. (The truth is, sexual experiences in relationships are not guaranteed: each person must consent.)

Even when slavery legally ended, negative messages about Black women's worth, value, position, and rights continued. From the early to mid-1900s, Black women were still made to stay home, cooking, cleaning, raising the children, and caring for the family. They may no longer have been enslaved, but in many ways they were not allowed to have the independence that men had.

There has long been an expectation that Black women will do what is needed and expected, with a smile on their face. They are expected to stay "strong," handle whatever family challenges come up, and tend to their family's needs. When you think about these messages—do they connect to your experience in the past and present?

In more recent decades, young Black girls have been taught to be polite, nice, quiet, and to stay away from arguments, conflict, or trouble—to avoid appearing as the "angry Black woman." If you experienced this growing up, then the idea of being nice, polite, and avoiding conflict was likely strongly instilled in you. Meanwhile, young boys are taught to be tough, firm, and stand up for themselves. Instead of staying away from conflict, they are taught to confront it head-on. For young boys, aggression is normalized, whereas for young girls it is condemned and deemed "unladylike."

These societal constructions of gender roles can translate into adult relationships where men are considered superior and women are expected to play a more subordinate role. Men are granted power over women—including over women's bodies—and even permitted to use force to discipline a woman who is out of their control. After all, the men were taught to charge and lead in their relationships, while women were taught to follow.

As you think back on your own childhood, are any of these messages familiar? What were you told about being a Black girl in the society you grew up in? What were you taught as you became a Black young woman? What messages about your place, and your worth, do you carry today? Take a moment to reflect on these and journal about your responses.

Power and Control

In the 1980s, the Domestic Abuse Intervention Program (DAIP) developed a tool to better explain how power and control manifest in domestic violence in relationships: the Power and Control Wheel (DAIP 2017). The image is not as important as the content, which shows the methods that abusers may use to exert power and gain control. The wheel contains eight types of abuse that can be found within domestic violence relationships.

1. *Coercion and threats.* An abusive partner may threaten to harm or kill you; they may also threaten to harm themselves or commit suicide. They might involve you in illegal activity, or make you engage in illegal activity and then hold it over your head.

2. *Intimidation.* An abusive partner may pull out weapons, destroy property, or use other actions to make you afraid.

3. *Emotional abuse.* An abusive partner may engage in name-calling, belittling, or otherwise attempting to make you feel bad or guilty. They may try to humiliate you or play mind games—for example, by making you feel that you were crazy for thinking that something had happened, also known as "gaslighting."

4. *Isolation.* An abusive partner may control who you can interact with. They may pick fights with your family and make you choose their side. They may then insist that you spend less time with your family or friends because of the conflict (that they created). They may also try to limit where you go or which friends you communicate with.

5. *Minimizing, denying, and blaming.* An abusive partner may shift responsibility for their abusive behavior, deny that their actions have occurred, or blame you (victim blaming) by saying you should have behaved differently to stop their abusive behavior.

6. *Using children.* An abusive partner may threaten to take your children away. They may try to make you feel guilty for wanting to leave and say that you are abandoning the children or tearing the family apart. They may even tell the children negative things about you.

7. *Using male privilege.* An abusive partner may take advantage of gender-role stereotypes that keep you feeling subservient.

8. *Economic abuse.* An abusive partner may restrict your ability to get money by withholding funds, making you ask for money, limiting your ability to work, or even taking money that is yours.

Overall, the Power and Control Wheel exemplifies how abusive partners use manipulative tactics to maintain a stronghold over the relationship. This, along with the gender-role stereotypes perspective, can be helpful for understanding complicated dynamics in domestic violence.

However, there are also important limitations to consider around these two perspectives. A focus on gender-role stereotypes can unintentionally assume that all relationships have opposite-sex partnerships, or that domestic violence only happens within opposite-sex relationships. We already explored that myth as untrue. Violence and abuse within relationships is not confined to male-female relationships.

Also, although there is typically a dynamic of an abusive partner trying to get and keep power by exerting control over a victimized person, it is also possible for both people to fight for power and for both to have some control. If only the abusive partner has power and control, does that mean that the victimized person has none? Is it possible for someone who is being abused or victimized to still find power or to have any control? We will explore this more in chapter 8, when we discuss recognizing your power and reclaiming control.

The Impact on Mental and Physical Well-Being

The constant threat to safety, living in fear, and walking on eggshells in the relationship can create a perpetual state of anxiety and angst. In this way, domestic violence poses a significant risk to a survivor's mental, physical, and social well-being.

Domestic violence often includes both violence that is threatened and violence that actually occurs—which can include serious injury or even death. These types of threats and actual violence are considered traumatic experiences, and can result in post-traumatic stress disorder (PTSD). Even witnessing such violence can be traumatic, which is why, in addition to considering the impact on you, it is also important to think about others (such as children) who might witness domestic violence.

Mental Health: In addition to outcomes of PTSD, Black female survivors have also shown mental health implications in the areas of depression, alcohol use, substance use, anxiety, suicide ideation, and anxiety (Lacey et al. 2015).

Physical Health: The NISVS survey also showed that people with a history of domestic violence reported worse physical health than those without a history of it. Specifically, there was a high occurrence of individuals with a history of domestic violence reporting asthma, irritable bowel syndrome, diabetes, high blood pressure, frequent headaches, chronic pain, difficulty sleeping, and activity limitations (Black et al. 2011).

Social Health: Additionally, as you read earlier in the chapter, domestic violence can include isolation, which impacts mental, physical, and social well-being. Having a support system is important for overall happiness, engagement, and life satisfaction. Without social support, one can experience even worse mental and physical health implications.

As with many aspects of our health care system, there are also notable inequities associated with Black women and domestic violence that can negatively impact overall health as well. For example, access to resources that are needed for leaving an abusive relationship are not equal within the US. Black people have been fighting for equal access to education, housing, employment, and health care for centuries. Black women continue to struggle with being ignored, even within the medical and mental health care system. Their pain is not always seen as pain. This can be true independent of their experience of domestic violence, and then the domestic violence situation can heighten it. Collectively, you can see the negative impact on your health as a Black woman survivor of domestic violence.

A Moment to Pause and Reflect

You have received a lot of information in this chapter. It's important to pause and check in with yourself as you digest everything. Thinking about domestic violence can be hard, and processing the information may bring up many emotions connected to your thoughts and past experiences—including ones that you might prefer not to have.

Emotions are okay. It's important that you allow yourself to feel them and to begin to understand them. Take time to think about the emotions that have come up for you. Grab your journal and write down whatever comes to mind.

As you approach the end of each chapter, we hope you will use these reflective moment activities to pause and reflect on what you learned, what you think, and how you feel. Journal on your responses before you move on to the next chapter.

This chapter's reflective moment begins with a breathing exercise. Use this exercise at any point as you move through the book, as you need it, before you answer the journal questions.

REFLECTIVE MOMENT: Breathing Exercise

Wherever you are lying or sitting, and in whatever way feels comfortable, take a deep breath in through your nose and then out through your mouth. Now, pause for a second. When you are ready, take another deep breath in through your nose and then out through your mouth.

Now, try to do that for three slow seconds. Breathe in for three seconds, and then out for three seconds. Do that a few times, and when you are ready, add in the statement "I am safe." Repeat this as many times as you need.

When you are ready, add in the statement "It wasn't my fault."

Breathe in for three seconds.... breathe out for three seconds.... say to yourself, "It wasn't my fault." Repeat this as many times as you need.

When you are ready, add in the statement "This is my journey to healing."

Breathe in for three seconds.... breathe out for three seconds.... say to yourself, "This is my journey toward healing." Repeat this as many times as you need, and when you are ready, move on to the journal questions.

Journal Prompts

1. What have you learned about domestic violence that you did not know before?

2. What did you know before, but you read in a new way or with a new understanding?

3. What information feels most important to remember for yourself?

4. What is most important to share with someone else?

CHAPTER 2

Intersecting Identities: Unique Struggles Faced by Black Women

The double jeopardy of being black and female in a racist and sexist society may well make one less afraid of the sanctions against success. A non-subservient black woman is by definition a transgressive—she is the ultimate outsider.

—Mamphela Ramphele

Because we are Black and women, we are automatically vulnerable to experiencing racism and sexism. Depending on where our other identities fall on the spectrum of privilege in American society, they can make us even more vulnerable to further devaluation and discrimination. This can happen because of being an older adult (ageism), having a disability (ableism), being poor (classism), loving the same sex (homophobia), having an outer appearance that does not match traditional notions of femininity (cisgenderism and transphobia), having nontraditional religious beliefs or practices (religious prejudice), or being born in different country (xenophobia). As a community, we are more likely than White people to be poor, we have lower rates of higher education, and we are more likely to have jobs that are detrimental to our health. These factors limit the choices and resources of Black women domestic violence survivors.

Our identities interact in complex ways, impacting how we cope with and heal from domestic violence. The lower-class Black woman in her sixties who identifies as heterosexual, Christian, and visually impaired will have a different experience healing from domestic violence than the twenty-two-year-old middle-class Black woman who identifies as transgender, is agnostic, and has been diagnosed with an intellectual disability.

The purpose of this chapter is to highlight complexities of domestic violence in our Black community, by exploring the various intersecting identities that Black women occupy, as well as how the sociopolitical climate in the United States can explain some of the experiences you may have as a survivor of domestic violence.

Age and Generational Influences

The stage of life you are in when you experience domestic violence will have a major impact on how you understand and heal from it. Studies show that abuse in Black romantic relationships can begin as early as middle school, though it is possible for abuse to begin sooner or later. A Black teenager who experiences domestic violence may not have the knowledge or language to label abusive behavior as domestic violence. And because there tends to be secrecy around domestic violence in our society, a teenager may just assume that this behavior is normal in relationships. As a result, a young survivor may remain in an abusive relationship longer than someone who is older and has been educated about how toxic domestic violence can be to a woman's overall health and well-being.

However, just being older doesn't make you immune to domestic violence. Domestic violence does not discriminate by age and being "older and wiser" doesn't mean you won't experience abuse by a partner. But as an older Black woman, you may encounter unique challenges navigating domestic violence because of your age. For example, you might be more prone to feeling ashamed for being in an abusive relationship, due to societal expectations that older people should "know better." This may feel especially true if you have adult children. Feeling shame may lead you to feel responsible for the abuse and make you less likely to speak up about it. Because most of the discourse, research, policy, and legislation around domestic violence focuses on younger women, if you are an older Black woman who chooses to seek support for domestic violence, you may receive inadequate support from community shelters, or may face sexist and ageist attitudes that overlook or delegitimize your experience. This could intensify feelings of shame and embarrassment.

Early Childhood Experiences

The interactions we witness between our parents as children can influence how we make sense of the abuse we experience. If you grew up in a household where you witnessed your mother being abused, you may view violent and controlling behaviors as normal, or even misinterpret them as a sign of love.

Witnessing abuse in childhood shapes the way we look at the world, how we behave with others, and the expectations we have for how people in relationships are supposed to act. If your father was controlling toward your mother, you might expect that the man's role in a relationship is to be in control and the woman's role is to comply, rather than challenge him.

If, as a child, you understood your father's jealousy as a sign that he loved your mother, when you are in a romantic relationship as an adult, you might assume your partner's jealousy is a sign that he cares for you, rather than a red flag. Since his behavior is not seen as a red flag, you might be prone to stay in that relationship, where you are vulnerable to further mistreatment. In this way, your upbringing can impact how you understand and respond to abuse in romantic relationships.

Abuse from a partner at an early age can lead to a pattern of abusive relationships in the future. Experiencing domestic violence as a teenager affects mental health issues such as anxiety, depression, posttraumatic stress, and lower levels of life satisfaction. The more abuse a Black girl experiences across her lifetime, the more vulnerable she is to the mental health consequences of domestic violence.

Age intersects with socioeconomic status to further complicate the picture. An impoverished teenage domestic violence survivor may face barriers to getting mental health treatment because her family has limited financial resources.

The way you view domestic violence is also impacted by the generation you belong to. With the popularity of movements like #MeToo and #WhyIStayed, although domestic violence is still disturbingly common, there is now widespread awareness that violence against women is problematic and socially unacceptable. This influences how millennials and younger generations understand, talk about, and cope with domestic violence.

Negative attitudes toward domestic violence might not be as common among Black women who grew up during a time when women had limited rights and were socialized into traditional gender roles. Because marital rape wasn't considered a crime in all fifty states until 1993, Black women from older generations may not realize that a husband forcing his wife to have sex against her will is abuse. This lack of knowledge can make older women less likely to tell anyone about their abuse and get the support they need.

Aside from difficulties talking about abuse, it can be difficult for older women to talk openly about sex, if they grew up in an era where talking about sex was taboo. A legacy of violence and unfair treatment may cause older women to distrust police, fear pressing charges against a violent partner, or not want to get involved with the US criminal justice system.

Many of us learn what is acceptable or unacceptable in relationships based on the relationships we witness and the lessons in womanhood we receive from the women in our families. If your grandmother and mother endured domestic violence, it is possible that abuse may be unquestioned, normalized, or seen as a burden that woman in your family are destined to bear. Some people describe this as a "generational curse."

A scene on the television show *How to Get Away with Murder*, starring actress Viola Davis, demonstrated how abuse can be normalized and passed down from generation to generation in Black families. In the scene, Viola Davis's character (Annalise) angrily confronts her estranged mother, whom she blames for not protecting her from her maternal uncle, who repeatedly raped Annalise as a child. As a heated argument ensues, Annalise's mother tells her that she is not the only one: that she (and other women in their family) suffered rape many times throughout her life—at the hands of a reverend, men she worked for, and men she dated. She went on to scold Annalise for talking about her childhood abuse and seeking therapy for it:

"I told you—men take things. They've been taking things from women since the beginning of time. Ain't no reason to talk about it and get all messy everywhere. Certainly, no reason to go to a head-shrinker for help and end up marrying him."

This scene also highlights the culture of secrecy around abuse and the stigma surrounding mental health treatment in the Black community. Annalise's mother made it clear that women should not complain about the ways they have been abused by men, nor should they seek help from a mental health professional (head-shrinker). If your mother had or has a perspective like Annalise's mother's, you might find it difficult to talk to her about your abuse, let alone leave the relationship.

Visible and Invisible Disability

Black women's experience of domestic violence can also be impacted by the presence of an intellectual, physical, or mental disability. Many women with intellectual disabilities report feeling devalued and rejected in childhood. These early childhood experiences can be a gateway to domestic violence when, yearning for acceptance, they find love and belonging in the arms of an abusive partner.

The stigma and bias in our country surrounding disability places women with disabilities at risk of being manipulated, taken advantage of (financially and otherwise), overlooked, and disbelieved when they report domestic violence. Internalized stigma can also make you more accepting of abusive behavior, if you fear your options for partners are limited because of your disability.

If you are a woman with a disability, lack of previous relationship experience and low awareness around what is socially appropriate or acceptable can make it difficult for you to identify abusive behavior, set boundaries with abusive partners, or leave an abusive relationship. If your intellectual disability makes it difficult to make sound judgments or decisions, this may have made you more vulnerable to being dominated or controlled by an abusive partner. Due to the nature of your disability, you may have found it difficult to communicate your abuse to family members, friends, or health care workers. This could have led you to remain in an abusive relationship for a prolonged period, or you may have received inadequate support.

Stereotypes surrounding disability in our society are harmful to survivors of domestic violence with disabilities. Nondisabled people in health care or law enforcement may inaccurately assume that, because of your disability, you are not likely to be taken advantage of sexually, or would be less severely impacted by domestic violence.

Even without a disability, due to stereotypes that were created to justify the enslavement of Black people, Black women today are still often considered immune to pain. As a consequence, we are more likely to have our pain dismissed by medical professionals, and less likely to receive proper medical treatment. These experiences can cause us to have less trust in the medical system, and can prevent survivors from seeking treatment when they need it most. If a health care worker or law enforcement official who served you held these problematic beliefs, you may find that you did not receive the level of protection, resources, or support that you needed.

Black women with physical disabilities can experience unique challenges in the context of domestic violence. In American society, the privileging of "able" bodies leads women with physical disabilities to be overlooked. This can make it difficult to secure employment, rendering you, as a Black woman with a physical disability, dependent on an abusive partner to meet your financial needs.

There are several problematic assumptions and myths about women with disabilities that increase their vulnerability to violence and abuse. For example, there is a notion that women with disabilities are unfit for parenthood and therefore unlikely to be in romantic relationships. Other problematic ableist and sexist assumptions are that women with disabilities shouldn't be taken seriously, or that they are asexual or not physically attractive. These problematic assumptions harm disabled Black domestic violence survivors, by making it harder to receive the care and resources they need to heal.

Black women who experience domestic violence usually suffer mental health effects: invisible disabilities that may not be immediately apparent, including depression, post-traumatic stress disorder, anxiety, and sleep problems. Studies show that Black women domestic violence survivors are more likely to experience poor mental health than White and Latina survivors, and the experience of racism while in a violent relationship further deteriorates their mental health.

When women lose consciousness from a blow to the head or being strangled by an intimate partner, they can experience long-lasting brain injuries that affect their ability to think and function in daily life— known as *traumatic brain injury*. Black women who have traumatic brain injuries are more likely to suffer from depression, post-traumatic stress disorder, and physical injuries that require hospitalization.

In the short term, this creates unique challenges for the Black domestic violence survivor without adequate insurance or access to mental health treatment. Black women who can afford mental health treatment may choose not to seek treatment, due to not trusting health care professionals, previous experiences of discrimination in health care settings, or fear of deportation, if the United States is not their home country. In the long term, untreated mental health issues among Black domestic violence survivors can get worse, and can even stop them from working, or limit their ability to properly take care of themselves and their families.

Disability often intersects with social and economic status, because people with disabilities are more likely to be poor and unemployed. In many cases, disabled women's economic disadvantage is due to broader structural oppression (e.g., inaccessible, rigid, and discriminatory workforce practices) that makes it more difficult for women with disabilities to secure gainful employment. The economic disadvantages faced by women with disabilities can create financial dependence on an abusive partner, making it more difficult to leave a violent relationship. On the other hand, a disabled woman with any level of economic independence may be a target of financial abuse.

Religion and Spirituality

Within the Black community, religion, faith, and spirituality are cornerstones. In decades past, the church was the only place where Black people could be leaders—and it is still a place of hope and refuge from the racism and violence Black people experienced in the world. Black domestic violence survivors who identify as religious (meaning they frequently attend religious services, watch or listen to worship services online or on the radio, pray, and/or read the Bible, Qur'an, or other religious books) often seek refuge in their faith community. Some studies show that church attendance makes Black women less likely to experience domestic violence. When a Black woman does experience domestic violence, church attendance and a supportive community can shield her from the negative mental health effects.

However, in some instances, religion can harm survivors of domestic violence, by worsening symptoms of depression and PTSD. For instance, one challenge Black women can face in the church is being told, either directly or indirectly, that they are somehow responsible for the abuse they experience. This might come in the form of questions about what was done to provoke partner abuse, or about how well a woman is living up to her duties as a wife. Being blamed for domestic violence has damaging mental health effects for women who are already more prone to suffer depression, anxiety, and post-traumatic stress disorder.

Many religions encourage followers to be forgiving, patient, and self-sacrificing. Being taught to put the needs of others above yourself and be long-suffering through trials may lead you to try and "stick it out" with an abusive partner, or feel compelled to forgive partners who are repeatedly abusive and not committed to changing their actions. The message of self-sacrifice from faith traditions might also lead you to feel like you're being selfish if you choose to leave an abusive relationship, especially if children are involved. If you've been taught that mental health symptoms signal a lack of faith, you might downplay the impact of domestic violence on your health and be less likely to seek treatment to heal from domestic violence. In many religious traditions, divorce is frowned on. As a religious woman, you may feel like you failed your faith or Higher Power by choosing to leave an abusive partner.

Church members or leaders who are uneducated about the nature of domestic violence might unintentionally condone domestic violence by making biblical excuses for abusive behavior, or by encouraging you to be submissive, pray, and have faith that things will get better. This type of advice can leave you vulnerable to repeated abuse or even death.

Independent of the advice you receive from church leaders, you yourself may cope with abuse by relying on spiritual principles. Some traditions teach that a Higher Power will fight our battles and punish people for their sins in the afterlife. If a survivor copes with domestic violence by believing that a Higher Power will ultimately punish an abusive partner, she may stay in a dangerous relationship.

Domestic violence can even negatively impact your relationship with God, Allah, or another Higher Power. If you prayed for a Higher Power to make the abuse stop, but it continued, you may feel abandoned or betrayed by God. If you have been taught that bad things happen to people as retribution for past sins, you could even believe domestic violence is God's way of punishing you—and, as a result, experience shame or guilt around that. In the aftermath of domestic violence, you might feel disconnected from God, which can result in feelings of loneliness, and can increase vulnerability to mental health issues like depression or anxiety.

Being Black in a White-Dominated World

The costs of domestic violence are different for Black women, compared to other groups of women. Experiencing racial discrimination makes Black women more likely to experience violence in their relationships.

One major health outcome associated with domestic violence in Black women is unintentional pregnancies. Black domestic violence survivors have many pathways to unintended pregnancy. First, compared to White women, studies have found that Black women rely more heavily on abusive male partners to make decisions about contraception (for example, choosing to wear a condom or not). This transfer of power to male partners leaves Black women vulnerable to sexually transmitted infections and other health consequences.

Second, Black women are more likely than White women to experience reproductive coercion in abusive relationships. Reproductive coercion is a type of sexual abuse in which an abusive partner restricts their partner's ability to make her own choices about pregnancy. Reproductive coercion ranges from flushing birth control pills down the toilet to removing a condom during intercourse without asking for permission.

Third, Black male partners of Black women are more likely to be deceptive about condom use, not wear condoms during intercourse, remove condoms during intercourse, or intentionally impregnate their partners. This behavior is often motivated by Black men's fear of mass incarceration and early death, due to high levels of violence in their communities. Due to the many disadvantages they face, some Black men don't believe they will live past the age of thirty-five, so they feel pressure earlier in life to leave a legacy through the children they produce.

Unwanted pregnancies pose unique challenges for Black women in violent relationships, because they may feel compelled to stay with a partner, may face financial challenges as a single parent, or may lack access to adequate medical care to ensure a healthy pregnancy. Moreover, for Black women who did not want children, an unintended pregnancy forces them to either accept motherhood or make difficult decisions like aborting an unwanted pregnancy or giving an unintended child up for adoption.

In violent relationships, Black women sometimes face a moral dilemma that is unique to being Black and a woman. The legacy of racism in the United States has negatively impacted Black men, through police brutality and mass incarceration. These factors can cause Black women with Black male partners to be hesitant to call the police or press charges when their partner is abusive. Unsure of whether Black men will receive fair treatment in the criminal justice system, many Black women face community pressure to keep their abuse silent.

Due to the oppressive treatment Black Americans face, you may have also struggled with the idea that talking about the abuse you experienced at the hands of a Black partner was betraying the Black race. In these instances, when you do not report abuse, you essentially "take one for the team"—but pay the price with your health, happiness, and, in the worst cases, your life. Remaining silent about abuse creates a lot of pressure. We hope this book helps you give yourself permission to speak your truth, despite the pressure to be silent.

The social construct of Black women as incredibly strong also creates unique challenges for Black domestic violence survivors. The conception of Black women as strong was formed by slaveholders, to rationalize their treatment of Black women. Over time, the Black community has taken on this ideal of Black womanhood, to resist the racism and sexism Black women face. The Strong Black Woman has several defining characteristics: she is capable of handling enormous amounts of pressure, and is self-reliant, emotionally reserved, and self-sacrificing.

If you were raised to be a "Strong Black Woman," this can influence how you cope with domestic violence. Rather than seeking treatment, you might power through the emotional and mental pain stemming from domestic violence, not realizing all the ways that it's impacting your functioning in daily life. Used to prioritizing others' needs above your own, you might find it difficult to leave an abusive relationship, perhaps because you're worried about the impact on your children. Family and community expectations that Strong Black Women "stick it out no matter what" may have led you to worry about how others will perceive you for leaving an abusive relationship. If you view yourself as a Strong Black Woman, you might also feel guilt or shame for being victimized, and you could be more prone to struggling with depression on your journey to healing from domestic violence. Through the practice tips we will provide in coming chapters, we hope to help you see it is okay to not always be strong, and that strength comes in many forms, including being vulnerable and acknowledging the impact domestic violence has had on you. It takes a different kind of strength to heal from domestic violence.

Finally, since Black women have not always been recognized by the law as victims of abuse, you might have been hesitant to report an abusive partner in the past, expecting that your allegations might not be taken seriously. This may have led to a pattern of unhealthy coping, such as suppressing or stuffing your emotions, trying to numb emotions with sex, physically harming yourself (e.g., cutting, hitting, burning, or punching yourself), or binge-eating.

Negative racial stereotypes that originated to justify the enslavement and objectification of Black women still exist today, and they can negatively affect attitudes toward Black female domestic violence survivors and the level of care they receive. Stereotypes that paint pictures of Black women as angry, bossy, controlling, hyper-sexual, and difficult to get along with may cause family and friends to question the validity of a Black woman's domestic violence claims, or even blame her for the violence she has endured.

Worse, these negative stereotypes can influence how law enforcement, attorneys, or health care professionals respond when a Black woman reveals she has experienced domestic violence. Negative responses to survivors (e.g., blame, treating the victim differently) intensify PTSD symptoms, encourage use of unhealthy coping strategies (e.g., denial, self-blame, abuse of alcohol and drugs), and make survivors feel less in control of their recovery from sexual assault.

Social and Economic Status

Black women are more likely to be impoverished because of the multiple forms of oppression they face, and domestic violence is more common among couples dealing with poverty. Living below the poverty line creates various disadvantages, like being reliant on public assistance, unemployment, living in neighborhoods that are violent and lack resources, and being at risk of homelessness. Impoverished women in violent relationships are more likely to receive citations for activities that occur at their properties during domestic violence, and to receive eviction threats by landlords if they regularly call 911 during domestic disputes. They may lose their security and personal possessions because of eviction. And then, when Black survivors make it back on their feet financially, many have difficulty securing housing, due to previous nuisance evictions, which could make them ineligible for low-income housing. All these factors leave Black women vulnerable to prolonged abuse.

Your options for escaping and healing from a violent relationship are limited when you lack education and financial resources. Impoverished Black women might lack adequate legal representation, or have limited knowledge about resources available to them if they want a restraining order or to press charges against an abusive partner. Due to a lack of public health education about therapy and the importance of mental health, lower-income Black women may think therapy is for "crazy" people and avoid treatment, for fear of being viewed poorly by family and community members.

Domestic violence occurs across the board in the Black community; wealthy women face different challenges, based on their financial status. Wealthy women may worry about losing their financial status or loss of privacy if the police are called during a domestic dispute. As a wealthy woman, your desire for privacy and to maintain the lifestyle you have grown accustomed to may limit your willingness to use domestic violence support services (for example, from domestic violence agencies) and other community services.

Sexual Orientation

Your sexual orientation describes who you are romantically or sexually attracted to. The assumption that domestic violence only occurs in heterosexual relationships could not be farther from the truth. Black lesbians and bisexual Black women experience high rates of domestic violence, often reporting verbal, physical, and sexual abuse at higher rates than women who are only attracted to men. Many of the unique challenges faced by queer Black survivors are rooted in homophobia and the stereotypes that paint lesbian women as hyper-sexual.

The stress of being in a same-sex relationship in a homophobic society negatively impacts the quality of same-sex relationships, which increases the chances of being victimized. As a gay, lesbian, or bisexual survivor, you may not be able to rely on support from family and friends if you aren't "out" to your support system, or if you were rejected by your family due to your sexual orientation. Homophobia and victim-blaming may have led you to receive inadequate treatment if you sought medical, legal, or mental health support for domestic violence.

If you are a gay, lesbian, or bisexual survivor who has not told your family about your sexual orientation, you may choose not to seek protection from law enforcement if you fear being outed during the legal process and don't want to lose emotional or financial support from homophobic family members. And queer survivors can sometimes adopt homophobic beliefs about themselves, and may even feel as though they are to blame for the abuse, or undeserving of treatment or support after leaving a violent partner.

Gender Identity

Due to biases in research and health care practices, we know less about transgender people's experiences of domestic violence. The little that we do know confirms that transgender individuals experience high levels of domestic violence. There is also evidence to suggest that Black people whose gender is not predominately male or female (known as nonbinary) experience domestic violence.

As a Black transgender survivor of domestic violence, you may have some unique challenges. First, you may have experienced mistreatment from health care, legal, and law enforcement professionals, who may not have taken your reports of domestic violence seriously, or who may have even blamed you for the abuse you suffered. Second, because of transphobia in the Black community, you may have experienced such traditionally "safe havens" as churches, or domestic violence community services, as unwelcoming and/or emotionally unsafe. If you are a transgender survivor who has previously experienced poor treatment or bias in the medical or mental health system, understandably, you may have chosen not to use services that could have offered you physical safety or some other kind of support.

Finally, as a Black transgender woman, you may have been a victim of a hate crime, or may have been subjected to violence by sexual partners who were confused about their own sexuality or unwilling to come to terms with their attraction to transgender women. Such abuse adds a layer of emotional betrayal that women who are not transgender do not experience.

Nationality and Immigration Influences

Due to anti-immigrant bias that exists in the United States, immigrant, refugee, and undocumented Black domestic violence survivors face unique challenges and barriers. Immigration status often impacts one's education status, level of financial independence, and ability to access the American health care system for domestic violence–related medical and mental health needs. There may be language barriers or cultural differences that prevent you from understanding domestic violence, that affect your ability to communicate the effects of abuse to law enforcement or health care professionals, or that limit the extent to which you can benefit from domestic violence support services that are not culturally sensitive.

Caribbean and African cultures have different expectations for how men and women are supposed to act in relationships. If you are from a culture in which violence against women is acceptable, you may not be knowledgeable about domestic violence, the services available to you, or your legal rights as a survivor. If your culture prohibits divorce and you are married to an abusive partner, you might not consider divorce a viable option.

Cultural mandates compelling women to place the needs of others above themselves may cause African immigrant survivors of abuse to stay in abusive relationships for the sake of their children. You may also feel guilty for seeking treatment or disloyal for disclosing abuse or leaving an abusive partner. Because of the collectivistic nature of your culture, as a Black immigrant survivor, you may have relied on family living outside of the United States for emotional support. Due to their lack of knowledge about the dangerous nature of domestic violence and their cultural beliefs around marriage, you might have experienced the support they offered as unhelpful or they might have pressured you to stay with your abusive partner.

Reflective Moment

After having read this chapter, you may have a variety of feelings. You may feel overwhelmed by just how expansive you are, as a person who possesses various identities. You may be feeling a sense of pride in your identity. Or you may be coming to realize just how influential your identities have been on your experience of domestic violence.

However you have arrived to the end of this chapter, make space for yourself. You might even consider revisiting the Reflective Moment breathing exercise from chapter 1. This time, breathe into your identity and your sense of self.

Journal Prompts

When you are ready, grab your journal and, using the chapter subheadings as a guide (age and generational influences, visible and invisible disability, religion and spiritual orientation, socioeconomic status, sexual orientation, gender identity, nationality and immigration influences), describe your personal identity as a Black woman. Then consider the following journal questions:

1. How have your identities influenced your experience with domestic violence?

2. What cultural barriers have you faced on your journey to healing from domestic violence?

3. How has your cultural identity positively impacted your healing journey?

CHAPTER 3

Why Survivors Stay and How Survivors Can Leave

The true focus of revolutionary change is never merely the oppressive situations which we seek to escape, but that piece of the oppressor which is planted deep within each of us.

—Audre Lorde

At some point during your relationship, people may have asked you "Why don't you just leave?" This was certainly the case for Assayiah, who you met in chapter 1. People around Assayiah did not understand why someone as "strong," "smart," and "beautiful" as she was would not just change a bad situation. Perhaps you have wondered the same thing. Well, changing a bad situation is not as easy as it sounds.

In this book, we are discussing the multilayered and complex nature of abusive relationships—for example, how the isolation that you may have experienced makes changing the situation even more difficult. We are also starting to discuss the complexities of staying versus leaving. People may have asked you "Why don't you leave?" or "Why didn't you go the first time _____ happened?" You may have even asked your-self these questions. But these questions put the blame on you, when you are the person who was harmed. Although it is true that we all have control over our decisions, these questions do not grasp the com-plexity of the decision or the reality of the consequences.

There are myriad factors that make leaving a difficult and danger-ous undertaking. Asking the question "Why don't you leave?" makes it sound easy. But nothing about abuse is easy. Instead of reflecting on why you did not leave, let's think about what factors might have con-tributed to you initially staying, if you did.

Revisiting Power and Control

Many influences can keep you in an abusive relationship. Let's use the eight tactics from the Power and Control Wheel (see chapter 1) to examine how an abusive partner might try to maintain a stronghold over the relationship and make leaving unimaginably difficult for you.

Coercion and threats: Your partner may have used coercive tactics such as involving you in illegal activity, and then holding it over your head by threatening to tell the authorities or expose your involvement in other ways. The fear, worry, and anxiety that comes from having these threats hanging over your head can make you feel stuck and with limited options for leaving.

Your partner may have also threatened serious harm to you, themselves, or other people you care about. They may have threatened to kill you or themselves. Both types of threats can be terrifying. An abusive partner threatening their own life can make you believe that their safety and well-being are in your hands—that you are responsible for it. That is a manipulative tactic meant to keep you compliant with what they want. It is meant to keep you under their control and afraid of what would happen if you left.

Intimidation: An abusive partner might pull out weapons, destroy your property, or use other actions (e.g., physical violence) to make you fearful of them. These tactics can make the thought of leaving terrifying. Even in the absence of physical or sexual violence, intimidation can be used to create an emotional and/or spiritual weakening in you that hinders your ability to exercise the emotional strength and freedom that leaving requires. They can create a state of fear and anxiety around if, when, or how violence or other means of destruction might come your way—as with the use of threats.

Emotional abuse: Using emotional abuse to tear you down is an intentional effort to weaken your mindset, mental strength, and self-awareness, which are required to leave abusive relationships. For example, abusive partners play mental and emotional tricks to make you question your experience and even think it's not real. Perhaps there were times when you began to recognize or address the abuse and your partner pretended nothing was happening. They may have called you crazy for even thinking something happened. Making you second-guess your experiences leads to you questioning yourself and having less trust in your instincts. This type of tactic can lead to a shift in your trust: from your internal voice and instincts to your partner's external voice. This shift away from self-trust in your own experience creates a level of uncertainty in yourself that can influence the decisions around staying or going.

Isolation: When abusive partners control who you interact with, they isolate you not only physically but emotionally as well. The support systems that you had may be more removed from you, thereby making it more difficult to talk about your experiences with people you trust, or to receive their counsel. It is harder to leave on our own than it is to leave with the support of others. When isolation tactics are paired with emotional abuse, you might not have loved ones to remind you of your inner voice. Again, that makes building the strength and courage that it takes to leave extremely difficult.

Minimizing, denying, and blaming: Your partner might have shifted responsibility for their abusive behavior, denied that their actions occurred, or blamed you for their actions by saying you should have behaved differently to stop the abuse. Perhaps they said the abuse was an accident and that you were blowing it out of proportion. They may have even said that the relationship would be better if you changed your behavior. These tactics may have made you question the need to leave the relationship. Instead of leaving because your partner is abusive, you may have stayed because you felt responsible for their temper or because they convinced you that nothing was wrong.

Using children: Your children being used against you may be one of the hardest parts about being in an abusive relationship and about leaving it. A common tactic may have been for your partner to threaten to take your children away from you if you didn't conform to what they wanted in the relationship, or if you considered leaving. Perhaps these are children that you share biologically with your partner...perhaps these are children that you share with your partner through adoption, fostering, or other means of guardianship...or perhaps you do not share these children with your partner at all, but your partner still made threats about having your children taken away as they attempted to disprove your parenting abilities. They may have combined this with economic abuse (see below), assuming control over your finances to make caring for the child more dependent on them.

Another typical strategy is for an abusive partner to try to convince you that leaving would make you a bad parent. They may threaten to tell the children negative things about you, even things that are untrue.

This may further exacerbate the worry that your children will be taken away, or that the parenting relationship will be harmed by your leaving. Maybe they tried to convince you that your children need a two-parent household. Although it is common for people to desire a two-parent household, that image is predicated on a non-abusive, safe, and emotionally healthy environment. Abusive partners may try to make you believe a two-parent household with abuse is better than a one-parent household without it.

Using male privilege: Your partner might have forced you to engage in gender-role stereotypes that kept you subservient to them. As you saw with Assayiah, her partner, James, refused to let her continue her career, insisted she stay home as that was the "motherly" thing to do, and then also insulted her parenting and her ability to "take care of the home." He used the messages that Assayiah learned throughout life, about the expectations and job of a wife and mother, against her. Also, the gender-role stereotypes being forced on you may not fit how you see yourself. Similar to emotional abuse, enforcing these stereotypes can be a way of making you lose your sense of who you are, so you have to rely on your partner to tell you.

Economic abuse: Abusive partners come up with creative ways to limit your access to money that would allow you to leave the relationship. Whether it's restricting your ability to make your own money, monitoring how you spend your money, or withholding shared money from you, these behaviors make it hard to get your own housing, transportation, security systems, therapy, and other things that you need. When abusive partners limit your ability to work—by sabotaging jobs, interviews, or other employment opportunities—they also isolate you from potential support that you might find in a coworker. And again, if they also make you ask for their money, that diminishes your understanding of yourself as independent. Staying, at least temporarily, may then be tied to figuring out a way to gain more financial independence and save enough money to leave.

All of these tactics make you depend on your partner for something that is needed to leave the relationship. Thinking about them, we can understand how the abusive, manipulative, and strategic tactics by the abusive partner are big factors in what might have kept you with them.

Thoughts That Make Leaving Hard

Many societal messages that are communicated to us ultimately influence what we think about ourselves, others, and the world around us. *Cognitive theory*, which is about understanding how thoughts develop over time, is a good way to understand this influence. The theory suggests that, from a young age, you began to learn messages about how the world operates, who you are in the world, and how you should interact with others. In essence, the messages become internalized in you without you even thinking about it. They then influence how you feel (emotions), what you do (behavior), and even what you continue to think (thoughts).

These messages are things that you learned from parents, family, teachers, friends, and even from within society. They are tied to your culture and can be about your identities (e.g., Black, woman, spiritual, etc.). For example, you may have learned messages about strength, perseverance, harm, and reconciliation that can be connected to how you engage in relationships.

Strength and Perseverance

Black women have been conditioned to be strong, to take care of others, to keep up positive outward appearances, and to fix situations that need to be fixed. Throughout your life, you likely received messages about the strength, resilience, and determination of the Black woman. So many of these messages are positive. For example, through the media and in your own family, you probably saw Black women working multiple jobs, taking care of children, taking care of partners, building a home, thriving in their careers, and tackling any challenge that life brings their way. You learned that Black women can do it all and that "doing it all" shows great strength and perseverance.

However, doing it all and enduring whatever comes your way also has its challenges. It comes with the notion of suffering in silence, hiding pain, and being self-sacrificing. There is much responsibility placed on Black women to care for and address the needs of everyone else, even at the expense of themselves. Take a moment and think about your own experiences as a Black woman. How have you experienced the pressures and expectations in these areas?

As it relates to your relationships, these messages may have led you to think "I can fix them," or "I can help them change." If your partner engaged in the manipulative tactic of blaming and constantly told you that the abusive behavior was your fault, you might have internalized that sense of blame and truly began to take responsibility for fixing the abusive relationship. If you are also learning that Black women deal with anything that comes their way, then you may have believed that your partner's abuse was simply another thing you needed to deal with. Perhaps this notion of you being able to overcome anything led you to believe that an abusive relationship *was* something you could deal with. These societal messages of strength influence the decision to leave.

Harm and Reconciliation

Think about the messages that you have learned around harm and reconciliation. Remember that cognitive theory is about the way your thoughts develop over time and influence your actions and behaviors. If you were ever in a physical argument as a child, you likely learned about the importance of saying sorry and accepting apologies. If another child pushed you off the swing on a playground, an adult probably told that child to apologize to you. They might have also told you to accept the apology.

These are positive messages to teach children. However, in childhood, those messages do not allow for important context about when apologies should be made and when they should be accepted. There's not enough subtlety to allow for the understanding that every "I'm sorry" does not deserve an "I forgive you."

As a child, you may have been taught that you must accept someone's apology and forgive them. Most people internalize that message and engage in relationships with others with that understanding. That makes leaving an abusive relationship challenging.

Even as children learn that hitting and violence are wrong, they are still taught that an apology can fix the situation. Granted, the child who hits is also taught not to do it again. Even that message can lead to adults thinking that an abusive partner who says "I will never hit you again" might mean it. Or you might be more inclined to believe an abusive partner who says "It was an accident; I'm sorry."

You can likely see how internalizing these messages during childhood interactions makes for challenging adult interactions. As you have grown from a child into an adult, you continued to internalize these messages, and knowingly and unknowingly applied them in relation to other people. For example, you might have also told yourself that your abusive partner's apologies were enough and that they deserved your forgiveness.

Ideas around harm and reconciliation can also be connected to spiritual beliefs. Beverly Gooden, a social activist, began the 2014 Twitter conversation #WhyIStayed in response to a national conversation about domestic violence, which was sparked after a public display of violence between a football player and his partner. Gooden used #WhyIStayed to describe her personal situation of staying in an abusive relationship, and to invite others to also share their stories/reasons for staying. In one of her tweets, she shared that "I stayed because my pastor told me that God hated divorce. It didn't cross my mind that God might hate abuse, too."

The difficulty of changing these messages can be another thing that kept you in an abusive relationship, or at least made leaving more complicated. It's important to recognize them so that you can work to change them. We will discuss more about how to change these messages in later chapters of the book.

Emotions That Make Leaving Hard

In addition to thoughts about harm and reconciliation, emotions of fear, shame, embarrassment, and love also factor into decisions around leaving. Cognitive theory suggests that these emotions may be connected to thoughts that have developed over the course of your life. Along with our thoughts, our feelings, too, have been building over the years in ways that we may not have realized.

Fear

Leaving a relationship is one of the most dangerous times for any victim of abuse. You can likely recall thoughtfully assessing your fear, and carefully considering your options. Your partner may have been employing abusive tactics of threats and intimidation at that time. It would have been easy for fear to set in and for you to feel immobilized about leaving or moving forward.

Sometimes this immobilizing fear is also connected to the thought/saying "better the devil you know." Sometimes, it may feel easier to protect yourself from what you know than to protect yourself from the unknown.

For any individual, the unknown can be scary. And especially if you have experienced a level of emotional abuse that caused you to question your inner voice, or weakened your self-esteem or sense of self, then it is quite understandable that not knowing what will happen if you try to leave could produce fear that would make it even more challenging to leave.

Shame and Embarrassment

Shame and embarrassment are additional feelings that can be connected to messages you internalized. For example, you likely had (and still have) ideas of who you would be in a relationship with. These ideas may have come from watching relationships around you, including your friends' and family's relationships. Perhaps the relationships around you seemed strong, positive, and or even perfect. Without knowing the ins and outs of those relationships, including the hard times and challenges that were not outwardly shared, you can begin to feel a sense of shame and embarrassment if your relationship is not as "perfect" as someone else's.

It may also be that there were unhealthy relationships around you, and you heard others talk negatively about the people in those relationships. You may have recalled those messages when you thought about your relationship and felt a sense of shame and embarrassment at what people would think or say about you.

These internalized thoughts and feelings can even be derived from relationships that you may have watched on TV, in movies, or on your social media. Many TV shows and movies portray relationships in a particular way—perhaps with a two-parent household, as we discussed earlier, or perhaps where the couple faces the hardest challenge of life and are stronger together in the end. Sometimes, especially on social media, relationships are showcased in overly positive ways that might make you desire that experience. Shame and embarrassment can arise when your relationship does not match the positive portrayals of others'—or at the very thought of leaving your relationship, if it has been public on social media.

No matter where or how your expectations of relationships developed, they have had decades to form and solidify in your mind. When your life or relationships don't match up to what you expected of them, you might hide, for fear of what others will think. In that hiding, shame and embarrassment get even stronger, and the process of leaving gets even harder.

Love

The last emotion that can make leaving harder, and often the hardest for friends and family to understand, is love. You may have loved your partner, even with the abuse happening in the relationship. Perhaps some of your shame or embarrassment was also connected to that. It's cliché to say that love is a complicated feeling, but it's true.

Many abusive partners begin relationships in very loving and idealistic ways. The abuse may have developed over time—after so many months or years of dating, after you moved in together, or after you were married or committed in your partnership. It's often after the positive feelings have settled in that the true nature of the abusive partner begins to show. And love is not easy to turn off overnight.

Feelings of love can also complicate some of the power and control tactics abusive partners use. Take, for example, coercion and threats. In addition to not wanting to be harmed, you may also not want your partner to harm themselves. Those feelings of love, care, or concern that you had for your partner may strengthen your desire for them to stay safe, which you might see as meaning you staying.

Additionally, part of the love may be about the idea of what the relationship used to be, or what you perceived it still could be if the abuse would end. That type of love contains a sense of hope for change, which can influence the decision to leave as well.

Leaving Is a Process

We have spent time in this chapter exploring factors that go into the complex decision to stay; now, let's consider the factors that go into the difficult process of leaving. A *stages of change model* (Prochaska and Norcross 2001) can be helpful for exploring this, with its six stages of change: precontemplation, contemplation, preparation, action, maintenance, and termination.

Precontemplation: During the precontemplation stage, you may not have had much awareness that something needed to be changed. Most people are in this stage for months before any change begins. While in this stage, you may not have recognized or named that the relationship was abusive. Perhaps you viewed your relationship as unhealthy, but not quite abusive or something that needed to end.

Contemplation: Contemplation is the stage when you may have developed more insight that something in the relationship was problematic.

You may have begun to see the relationship as abusive. Likely you weren't ready to leave the relationship at this stage, but contemplating leaving would have become more present in your mind.

Preparation: In the preparation stage, you probably had a much better understanding of the abuse and decided to do something about it. You may have begun to take steps toward leaving: for example, reaching out to others, exploring and gathering your resources, or mapping out what leaving would look like. This may have been a time when you sought help from professionals or family and friends.

Action: Action is where you started taking steps toward leaving. Perhaps you purchased or rented a separate living space, moved out, or had your partner removed from your shared space. Perhaps this was a time when you changed the locks, changed your phone number, or broke up with your partner. This is a challenging stage to arrive at and can take at least six months, from Contemplation, to get to.

Maintenance: Maintenance is about actively maintaining the change that you created. You may be in this stage now. It's a very important stage. With any change, there can be a natural process of going back and forth. This stage of change acknowledges that change requires continuous effort to maintain. It would not be uncommon for you to constantly assess and reassess your decision to leave.

Termination: Termination is when people are never going back to what needs to be changed. In this stage, you may have left, moved on with your life, and feel ready to never look back. It feels wonderful to be in this stage, and it's also okay to be working toward it.

Some people say that this stage seems impossible. Abusive partners can make it very difficult. It can be hard to move on if an abusive partner is still displaying abusive behaviors—for example, stalking you when you are separated, or continuing to use your children against you. It's important to remember that not all abusive relationships end when you leave. You may be working toward leaving in a time frame that is specific to your situation.

As you already know, change does not happen overnight. Leaving an abusive relationship is a process that begins long before the decision to leave is made. When people ask "Why don't you just leave?" they're not understanding the complexity of the situation or the change process. The stages of change usually occur over a significant amount of time. You may move forward to one stage, and then back to another.

You may have made the difficult decision to leave and are now engaged in the difficult process of leaving. That is something to be very proud of. Take a moment to think about your experiences and how they may fit with the stages of change.

As you reflect on your experiences with change, it's important to also acknowledge that you should not have had to be the person to create change. You should not have been abused at all. It was not your fault; you didn't deserve it; and there is nothing that you did to make it happen. The responsibility of the abuse was and is on your partner. They should have taken responsibility for their actions and stopped being abusive. They should have recognized that their actions were harmful, and that they needed to leave. Unfortunately, abusers rarely do that, and so you were put in the position of needing to create change.

Reflective Moment: Processing Your Experience

Take a moment to sit with your thoughts and emotions as you close out this chapter. Maybe you connected with some examples that you have read here. Perhaps it brought up memories and reminded you of your experiences. Or perhaps you are reminded of something that was not covered here. What emotions do these memories bring up? What do you need at this moment? Engage in your breathing exercise as you reflect on these questions and consider your process of leaving.

Throughout this chapter, you read a lot of information about staying, and about leaving. A key takeaway is that there was a lot that went, or will go, into your decisions to stay in or leave your relationship. Manipulative tactics related to power and control were a means of keeping you in the relationship. Mental and emotional influences also contributed to your decisions. The decisions took time and were a process that couldn't occur instantly. You didn't "just leave" because staying is a complicated experience and leaving is a complicated process.

The healing journey is also a complicated process. We ask that you be patient with yourself and stick with the readings and exercises. It can be common to want to skip over some of the journaling exercises, but they are meant to provide space and opportunity to process your thoughts and emotions in a way that is important for healing.

Journal Prompts

1. How has your understanding of leaving an abusive relationship changed after reviewing this chapter?

2. What were some of the factors that contributed to your decision to stay or to leave?

3. What information from this chapter feels most important for you to have yourself or to share with someone else?

CHAPTER 4

Building Safety

Freeing yourself was one thing, claiming ownership of that freed self was another.

—Toni Morrison

In experiencing an abusive partner, you may have questioned why you couldn't keep yourself safe, or what else you could do to stop the abuse from happening to you. You likely tried everything that you could think of to reduce the risk of being harmed; however, as you may have learned, we cannot control someone else's behavior. What we can do is change the messages of safety that we learned early on in life and may understand to be true today.

In the last chapter, we explored how messages and thoughts of strength, perseverance, harm, and reconciliation developed over time and would have influenced your process around leaving your abusive relationship. Now, we'd like you to think about messages of safety you received, early in your life, and how that influences your current understanding of what it means to be safe.

Do you remember when you first learned to cross the street? Someone likely held your hand and taught you to look both ways. In general, this is an important lesson to teach any kid. In fact, it's a common lesson that is taught around the world and practiced in all types of settings (home, school, daycare, etc.). The message is about safety. You were explicitly taught that looking both ways can keep you safe.

Childhood lessons often share an intentional, explicit message and an unintentional, implicit message. The unintentional, implicit message about looking both ways before you cross the street is about control. It says that if you look both ways, then you have some control over your safety.

That is partially true. What part of crossing the street can you control? You can look both ways. Which part is out of your control? You cannot control the cars on the street, or the drivers inside them.

In this way, safety can be talked about in terms of reducing your risk of being harmed. You usually have the potential to reduce your risk of harm, but if there is another person in the equation, you can't fully control your safety. Sometimes, people look both ways before crossing the street, and the danger they tried to avoid still comes out of nowhere. Sometimes, danger still comes on the quietest of streets, where it's least expected, and where many precautions have been taken. In this way, your safety is not fully in your control, but there are things that you can do to increase your chances of safety.

You can probably also recall messages about not running with scissors in your hand, or not touching a hot stove. These messages, too, are meant to protect you from being harmed or injured. They also teach you about vigilance, caution, and most of all, safety. Preventing harm by not running with scissors or not touching the hot stove may be more in your control, as there are fewer unknowns involving other people's behaviors.

These examples highlight the need for balance in understanding that control over your safety differs depending on the situation. As you explore building safety in this chapter, keep in mind that you have less control in some situations and more control in others.

Safety as a Black Woman

In an ideal world, safety would be the same for all people, regardless of their identity. Unfortunately, the world is not always ideal, and safety is not always equally available to people across the spectrum of diverse identities. Let's take a moment to consider what safety has meant for you, as a Black woman.

- What comes to mind when you think about the safety of Black people in your hometown or neighborhood?

- What about the safety of Black people within the greater context of the US?

- What messages have you learned about being safe as a woman?

- Has your understanding of safety as a Black woman changed over time, or remained the same?

Notions of safety for Black people have been a point of discussion for centuries. From hundreds of years ago, up to the present moment, there have been conversations about if Black people are safe, where Black people are safe, and what jeopardizes Black people's safety. Black families have had to engage in conversations about how to maintain their safety in a world where their safety is not guaranteed. Again, these are messages that start in childhood and continue into adulthood.

In your life, early conversations may have been about managing safety in certain places, such as a store or a neighborhood. Those conversations typically include directions to stay physically close to your parents (or another trusted adult), and not to talk to strangers. In later years, those conversations may have turned into messages about managing safety within society as a whole. Specific conversations may have included managing safety while being pulled over by the police.

Safety conversations occur for girls and women in a way that is different from the safety of boys and men. As a young girl, you may have received instructions about keeping yourself safe: for example, to walk in groups, watch your surroundings, be careful at parties, not leave your drink unattended, and more. As a woman, you might have also received messages about protecting your family and keeping them safe. As a Black woman, those lessons can be tied to the caretaking role of keeping the Black family (including the abuser) safe from a world that can be especially dangerous for Black people.

The conversations that Black families have about safety are critically important. They might have also left you conflicted about how to keep yourself safe, when your own safety seems to be in conflict with keeping your family safe. Take, for example, Yasmine's situation.

One evening, Yasmine and her partner, Jayden, were going to get something to eat. Jayden was driving and their baby was in the back seat.

Out of nowhere, Jayden began questioning Yasmine about men she worked with and if she ever ate lunch with them. Yasmine explained that many people eat lunch together, depending on who is available that day. Jayden became enraged and tried to kick Yasmine out of the car. At one point, Jayden went over to the passenger's side of the car and began physically pulling Yasmine out of the car. People were stopping and watching in horror. Yasmine was humiliated.

Having done nothing wrong, and being in the middle of the street, Yasmine refused to get out. Jayden eventually pulled her out of the car. She was scared for herself and her child.

This situation went on for long enough that the police arrived. Yasmine was grateful that someone on the street called them, but when she saw them, and looked at her Black family, she was also terrified.

At first, you might think that Yasmine's life was in danger because of Jayden's actions. That was true for her, and it was scary. Her child was also in the car, which was also terrifying to her. However, to Yasmine's surprise, once the police arrived, she was also scared for Jayden. In that way, she feared for all of their safety.

This situation occurred during a time when protests against the murders of Breonna Taylor and George Floyd were at their highest. Breonna Taylor was a Black woman from Kentucky who was killed by police after they forced entry into her apartment, looking for her boyfriend. George Floyd was a Black man from Minnesota who was killed by police who kneeled on his neck for more than nine minutes. There were many more deaths of Black women, men, and children that ran through Yasmine's mind. She thought of Tamir Rice, a twelve-year-old Black child in Ohio who was killed by police when they shot him in a park for playing with a toy gun.

Would the police help her and her child, or would she, or they, be killed? Would Jayden survive an arrest, or would he die in police custody? Would her child lose a parent? Yasmine felt conflicted about whether she was safe from her abuser, and from the people who had come to help.

No one should have to experience this dilemma, but these are the complexities that Black women face. When you call for help, you deserve to receive help and to feel safe with the help that is coming. You deserve to know that you will be protected and not harmed. You deserve to consider your safety and the safety of your child, above and beyond the safety of an abusive partner. Again, in an ideal world, safety should be the same for all people, regardless of their identity. Unfortunately, for Black women, that is not always the case.

Again, please consider these questions: How has your understanding of safety been influenced by your identity as a Black woman? What does safety mean to you?

Disrupting or Confirming Messages About Safety

Abuse in a relationship can disrupt or confirm your understanding of being safe in the world. During your upbringing, you likely held one of two messages about safety: one that revolved around the world being a safe place, and the other that revolved around the world being a dangerous place. If you saw the world as a safe place, then you probably saw yourself and others as safe in it. However, if you saw the world as a dangerous place, then you likely believed that you were not safe in the world, or safe with people in the world.

Abuse can disrupt your understanding of safety by changing how safe you feel. Maybe you previously felt a general sense of safety in the world, but the trauma and abuse made you feel the opposite. Maybe now you feel unsafe. Trauma and abuse can also confirm messages of being unsafe. Perhaps you have always thought that the world was a dangerous place, and that people could harm you. In that case, abuse in a relationship might have confirmed that message, as another example of someone hurting you.

Take a moment to consider if your understanding of safety has been disrupted or confirmed through abusive experiences. Also, as you reflect on your understanding of safety, ask yourself: Does this understanding apply solely to one relationship or experience? Or is it a part of a larger narrative about safety in general?

One challenge with your experiences with safety is that the lessons you learned can become ingrained in your thinking and, potentially, overgeneralized to other parts of your life. They can begin to apply to situations outside the specific one they began with. If you believed that you were not able to keep yourself safe in your previous relationship, then that message might overgeneralize to other relationships where you might also believe that you cannot be safe. If you thought that you were supposed to keep yourself safe but were not able to, then that message might overgeneralize to you thinking that you will never be able to keep yourself safe.

Each situation is different, and although it's important to learn lessons that you can apply to other aspects of life, it's also important to maintain balance, so that those lessons don't become overgeneralized and applied to every possible situation. Applying them to every situation could make you feel very unsafe in the world. Later in this chapter, we will learn more about strategies to avoid overgeneralization.

Will I Ever Be Safe Again?

Despite feeling scared, uncertain, and unsafe in an abusive relationship, you have worked, and may still be working, to find your way through it and survive. Finding your way through is a process. As you continue on the path toward healing, ask yourself: What would it mean to feel safe again? Is that a real possibility?

Safety is about more than just the physical absence of danger. Even when you are away from danger, you might naturally still feel unsafe. That's normal. Although a part of safety is about physically being safe, unharmed, and unthreatened, another part of safety is about the feeling of being safe. It's about having a sense that you are safe in the world, safe from dangerous people, and safe within yourself. That is a sense of safety that you can work toward feeling again.

One thing that might make you question your sense of safety is fear that your future relationships will also be abusive. You might experience a generalized thought that you were unsafe in your previous relationship and so you will always be unsafe in other situations or relationships. Again, generalizing your experience is not an abnormal thing to do. In fact, you likely do it in many aspects of your life, and it can be self-protective at times.

For example, when you learned not to run with scissors, you likely generalized that message from one pair of scissors to all pairs of scissors. You probably then generalized it to any object that is sharp or pointy; you probably don't run with knives. Here, you generalized a message in a way that is self-protective, which is helpful.

But if you overgeneralized the message to mean that you should never run with anything in your hand, then your life would be more limited and driven by your fears around safety. You would be unable to participate in a relay race and pass the baton in grade school, carry your phone in your hand while on a jog, or hold on to your coffee as you ran to catch a departing bus, train, or flight.

A part of the reason we don't want to overgeneralize the message is because the specific context of the message may be different in each situation. You will hesitate to run with scissors, but also feel safer running with the plastic scissors that are made for children, given the context of the scissors (they are plastic), the context of yourself (you are an adult, who is more careful than a child), and the probability of danger (you are unlikely to be seriously harmed by plastic).

Instead of overgeneralizing your understanding of safety (or lack of safety), see if you can consider the context and respond in a way that matches it. This is also true for relationships with others. As you learn about your safety in relationships, you are exploring important messages about what it means to be safe. Take a moment to consider some questions.

- What have you learned about safety, from your experiences in an abusive relationship?

- What messages about safety are you carrying with you today?

- Do you see those messages playing out in other types of relationships that are not romantic? For example, what do you think about safety with family or friends?

Rather than generalizing thoughts about safety to any and all relationships, use the next section as a tool to consider how you might judge your safety in each relationship that you encounter. It can be challenging to hold on to lessons you have learned, while also judging each situation separately, but it's also one strategy to build a sense of safety.

Building a Sense of Safety

You might be wondering how you can begin to feel safe again when your safety has been threatened. Following are some strategies you can consider and practice as you think about what safety looks like within relationships, which aspects of safety are most important to you, and what type of relationship you want to build from here.

Developing Awareness of Safety: Raising your understanding about safety in relationships can help you become more aware of what a healthy, non-abusive relationship can look like. Think of this strategy as the foundation for building a safe relationship. You must know what safety is before you can build a relationship around it.

EXERCISE: Components of Safety

To start, reflect on the different types of relationships you have had throughout your life. Consider your family and social relationships, in addition to your romantic ones. Which relationships did you feel safe in? What was it about these relationships that led to a sense of safety? Perhaps it was the evidence that you were not harmed. Perhaps it was the love, care, and protection that you received. Or maybe it was knowing that the person was respectful, reliable, and accountable to you. In your journal, list the specific relationships that come to mind, and also identify what felt safe about them.

It can be challenging to assess what safety looks like in a relationship. Every person is different, and their specific needs, including what makes them feel safe, can be different. However, there are some common concepts that exist across safe relationships. Consider the following list. What do each of these words mean to you?

- Respect
- Trust
- Safety
- Accountability
- Nonviolence
- Freedom
- Autonomy

- Empathy
- Compassion
- Validation
- Support
- Equality
- Love

When you thought about what felt safe in your relationships, did any of these concepts come to mind? What was present from the list? What was missing? Use your journal to add additional words that describe important aspects of your safety. As you move on to the next strategy, continue to reflect on these common concepts of safety in relationships.

Finding a Balanced Viewpoint: This strategy is about reshaping your thoughts about safety, to find a more balanced approach. The process of replacing unhelpful thoughts with helpful ones can lead to your desired change. Specifically, you can work to replace the unhelpful and overgeneralized messages about safety with other messages that will help you move toward building safe relationships. For example, you may change an overgeneralized thought of "I am not safe in *any* relationship" to a more helpful thought of "I am physically safe in this relationship and I am building greater emotional safety in other relationships."

Before you can change the overgeneralized thoughts, you must first be able to recognize them. Typically, overgeneralized thoughts contain words like "all," "always," "never," "nothing," "absolutely," "impossible," etc. What do you notice about these words? They are extremes. These words are not likely to be connected to thoughts that support a middle ground or a balanced perspective. An example of an overgeneralized thought might be "I am *never* safe."

Exercise: Finding a Balanced Viewpoint

Finding a balanced viewpoint requires that you ask yourself a few questions to see if you can find a more balanced and helpful viewpoint. Here are four questions to consider about a given viewpoint:

1. Is this statement fully true, with 100 percent accuracy?

2. Is this statement always true, 100 percent of the time?

3. What evidence am I basing this statement on?

4. Are there any examples where this statement might not be true, or where it's slightly different?

After you ask yourself those questions, consider if you should replace the extreme word with a word that is more balanced. For example, the word "never" is on the extreme end of "always." The word "sometimes" is in the middle. What would happen if you changed the statement "I am never safe" to "I am sometimes safe"? Consider how those statements feel different for you. Do they allow you to think about your current and future relationships any differently?

As you reflect on your thoughts about safety, the strategy of finding a balanced viewpoint allows you to identify the parts of your thoughts that may be unhelpful (perhaps they are the overgeneralized ideas), and find more helpful ways to view them.

This may sound easy, but it can be very hard. Be patient with yourself, and remember to use the four questions to gently challenge and explore your own thinking. Doing this can open space in your thinking and help you to find a more balanced approach for rebuilding your sense of safety.

Reconditioning Your Thoughts: Here's a strategy that can be helpful to use once you identify your new, and more balanced, thoughts. You have already learned how thoughts develop over time and influence your emotions and behaviors. To recondition your thoughts, it may help to have a process of continued reminders that the old thoughts you once held are done, and there are new thoughts that need to settle in and have a more positive influence on your goal of safety. In this process, you put cues around you, to remind yourself of important information that helps you move toward healing—for example, that you are safe, or that you can have a safe and healthy relationship again.

As you work to develop helpful thoughts about safety, you can write them down and place them around your home as reminders. In the same way that you developed ideas over time from family, friends, and society, you can also develop ideas over time from yourself.

EXERCISE: Positive Affirmations

Let's try an example.

Grab a few Post-its or index cards, if you have them; any kind of paper will also do just fine. Your journal can be used for now, but you should transfer the writing to a different piece of paper later on.

1. On separate sheets, write down the names of people who you felt safe in a relationship with.

2. Write down the statement that you developed during the Balanced Viewpoint exercise—the one that was a more balanced view of "I am never safe."

3. Write down one component of a healthy relationship that you wish to have. If you want, you can choose a word from the table you worked on for the Components of Safety exercise.

Place the Post-its/index cards/sheets of paper somewhere you will see them on a regular basis: for example, on the bathroom mirror, on the refrigerator, or in your car.

You can continue to add more notes as you work through this book. Each time you develop a thought that helps you move forward, or you have a memory that makes you feel one step closer to healing, write it down and place it where you can see it. Let it serve as a reminder that helps you combat the negative messages that may be easier to remember, and sometimes also more deeply ingrained.

Connecting to Healthy Relationships: You have already identified relationships in which you felt safe. Did any current relationships come to mind? Are there any supportive people who can encourage you in this process (or aftermath) of leaving the abusive relationship? Change and healing are both difficult processes and are rarely done in isolation. Having support can be vital to your ability to move forward and feel safe again.

Remember that safety is emotional, in addition to being physical. In addition to physically being safe, you likely desire emotional safety with others. Emotional safety requires empathy, care, compassion, and maybe even protection, when you are vulnerable. Connecting to the emotional safety that is present in your relationships (be they with friends, family, or partners) can increase the overall sense of emotional safety that you feel across relationships. Who are you in a healthy relationship with? Who in your village of supports makes you feel safe and reminds you that safety is attainable?

As you read in chapter 1, abusive partners may try to isolate you from friends and family who want to support you and remind you of what safety feels like. If you are now disconnected from some of the relationships where you once felt safe, then consider that rebuilding safety may also mean rebuilding those relationships. Of course, that may be easier said than done.

Throughout this book, you will learn about overcoming shame, embarrassment, trust issues, and other things that may make reconnecting to people difficult. Allow those lessons to help you rebuild relationships that are important to you, especially those where you felt safe.

Processing Your Experience

We've reflected a lot on safety in this chapter. You considered questions about how you developed an understanding of safety throughout your life. You reflected on your experiences of feeling safe in other relationships. You began to explore what it means to assess your safety and to rebuild a sense of safety with others.

As you finish this chapter, take a moment to engage in the following exercise of safety-building within yourself (versus in relationship to others). This safety-building is based on grounding exercises, which are one way of connecting with your body and reminding yourself when you are currently safe.

You may find that your mind wanders back to the abuse you experienced. Your thoughts may return to that previous time, and you may begin to feel that you are in danger in the present moment. When you feel scared, stop for a moment, and consider if this feeling of being scared is a warning to you that something is coming, if there is something truly wrong. Are you in danger? Or are you safe in that moment, simply remembering past moments when you were not safe?

Grounding techniques are one way to bring yourself to a calm state, so you are better able to assess your present experience. Most grounding techniques involve some tactile activity: for example, feeling the weight of your feet on the floor, your body in the chair, your hand on your legs, or your fingers on the pages of this book. The tactile piece of grounding is important because it brings your attention (and your mind) back to your body, which can help regulate a sense of calmness.

REFLECTIVE MOMENT: Safety-Building Grounding Technique

1. Sit comfortably with your feet on the ground. If you can, remove your shoes so that you can truly feel the ground beneath you. Run your feet back and forth across the floor. Notice what the ground feels like beneath your feet. Continue this for a moment and notice the temperature of the floor. Is it warm or cold? What is the texture?

2.   Bring your attention to any sound you hear as your feet glide back and forth. What is the sound of your feet sliding across the floor?

3.   Now, wiggle each of your toes. Try to wiggle them one by one if you can. Notice which toes are easier to move. Try to feel each one of them.

4.   Press the heel of your foot into the ground, and then your toes, and then your heel, and back to your toes again. Continue repeating this for a few more seconds. What does it feel like to flex your foot this way?

5.   Take a deep breath, then exhale. Try to breathe in for five counts and then out for five counts. Remind yourself of where you are and that you are safe there.

6.   Say to yourself, "I am freeing myself from what keeps me captured" or "I am doing the work to free myself, even from what is internal."

Journal Prompts

1.   What was the grounding exercise like for you?

2.   How have your thoughts about safety changed after reviewing this chapter?

3.   Which strategies did you find most helpful to consider, and which are you willing to commit to working on over the next week?

CHAPTER 5

Learning to Trust Yourself and Others

Quiet the opinions, expectations, pressures, demands, insecurities so you can hear your heartbeat. Then you will know...

—Thema Bryant, PhD

When we enter a romantic relationship, there are certain presumptions we make about our partner. Two of the most basic presumptions we make are that our romantic partners: 1) have our best interests in mind; and 2) will not purposefully harm us with their words, intentions, or actions. In making these presumptions, we extend them trust—we are confident that they care for our well-being, and we choose to make ourselves vulnerable to them.

In an ideal world, trust grows over the course of a relationship, as our partners display commitment, predictable and reliable actions, emotional vulnerability, genuine care, and attentiveness to our needs and desires.

Changes in trust over time are driven by experiences of violation and validation of trust. When people validate our trust by behaving in trustworthy ways, trust grows. When trust is violated, trust declines. The potential for trust to grow depends on the regularity, amount, and range of experiences that either confirm or disconfirm trustworthiness.

How Trust Is Impacted by Domestic Violence

The uncertain and unpredictable circumstances of abusive environments often prevent trust from maturing. Trust can be risky, because it opens the door for someone to be violated or betrayed. Domestic violence is a blatant violation of trust. Perpetrators are very good at earning your trust and getting you to rely fully on them. Then, over time, they begin to change.

Many abusers have two sides to them. An abuser who is extremely kind, thoughtful, and affectionate can also be a source of extreme pain and humiliation. This unpredictable behavior may be hard for you to wrap your mind around. Abusers manipulate you into believing that no one else loves you as much as they do, or that you'll never be able to find another partner who will respect and support you as much as they do. This is all a part of their strategy.

Abusers want to get you into a place where you don't fully trust yourself—because trusting yourself is empowering and can lead you to stand up for yourself or leave the relationship. Because of the mixed messages and manipulation, domestic violence can cause you to question everything you thought you knew about other people, yourself, and the way that the world works. If you previously believed people were generally trustworthy and could be relied on, domestic violence can cause you to be "on guard" around others and constantly question their motives.

Domestic violence can also cause you to lose faith in yourself. Because it's common for domestic violence survivors to be blamed for provoking or not stopping the abuse, you may come to see yourself as weak, incompetent, irresponsible, or stupid.

Finally, assumptions you might have had about mutual respect in relationships or your invulnerability to abuse may be shattered by domestic violence, causing you to now view the world as unsafe and unpredictable. There is also the possibility that domestic violence simply reinforces previously held beliefs. This is particularly true if you have a history of childhood abuse or neglect: you may enter relationships expecting to be disappointed, hurt, or lied to, only to have those expectations confirmed by an abusive partner.

Regardless of whether domestic violence shattered or confirmed your previously held assumptions, it can make it difficult to trust in future relationships. Because of the emotional, physical, and psychological pain you have endured, to protect yourself from future harm, you may tend toward complete distrust of others. On the other end of the spectrum, you may tend toward trusting others too quickly and overlook "red flags" suggesting that a person or situation is unsafe. Both rigid ways of approaching relationships (distrust, or blind trust) can create challenges. If you are extremely distrusting of others, it strains relationships, and you could be robbing yourself of the opportunity to experience happy and healthy relationships with family, friends, and future partners. If you are overly trusting, you could be at increased risk for being hurt or taken advantage of in future relationships.

Domestic violence makes it difficult to accurately judge the trustworthiness of a person or a situation. It may feel safest to stay in the extreme of "trust no one" (or, less likely, "trust everyone"). Yet it's nearly impossible to completely distrust everyone for the rest of your life.

We were not meant to do life alone. Black women are community oriented. We thrive, grow, and succeed in community. At the same time, not everyone *is* worthy of our trust. That's why it's important to learn how to assess the trustworthiness of others and allow your actions to be driven by this assessment, as opposed to allowing hurts from the past to cut you off from the healthy relationships you deserve. In this chapter, our goal is to teach you practical skills for assessing the trustworthiness of others and learning to trust yourself.

Why Trust Is Important

To trust is to choose to have faith in the reliability and integrity of a person or organization. According to University of Houston professor Brené Brown, who has been a guest on Oprah's Super Soul Sessions, there are seven qualities or requirements for trustworthiness: boundaries, reliability, accountability, vault, integrity, non-judgment, and generosity.

- To trust someone, we need our *boundaries* to be known and respected.

- We need to be able to rely on their word and know that they will consistently and *reliably* do what they say they will do.

- When trust is present, we are *accountable* to one another, and we each feel safe enough to make mistakes, own our mistakes, apologize, and make amends.

- When we trust someone, we feel secure in sharing our secrets, knowing that they will be held in confidence, like a *vault* safely stores valuables.

- We are more likely to trust people who display *integrity* by choosing courage over comfort, consistently doing the right thing (instead of the easy thing), and living a life guided by morals and values.

- We trust people who we can ask for help and be ourselves around without feeling condemned or *judged,* and we allow them to do the same.

- Finally, in trusting relationships, we give each other the benefit of the doubt. That is, when something important is forgotten, a mistake is made, or something hurtful was said, we make *generous* assumptions about the other's intentions—and they extend us the same grace when we mess up.

There are different types of trust: trust in ourselves, trust in other people/organizations, or trust in our theories of how the world works (e.g., the notion that good things happen to good people and bad things happen to bad people). When we trust in ourselves, we have confidence in our ability to make sound decisions. When we trust in people or institutions, we feel safe, comfortable, cared for, and we view them as dependable. When we trust in our ideas or theories of how the world works, we have a sense that the future is predictable, and, rather than believing everything is completely outside of our control, we understand that our actions play a role in shaping how our lives unfold.

Trust is important because it guides us to make choices in daily life that keep us safe, healthy, and happy. In relationships, trust helps us feel connected, confident, and comfortable.

Unique Experiences of Black Women with Trust

"The most disrespected person in America is the black woman. The most unprotected person in America is the black woman. The most neglected person in America is the black woman."

—Malcom X

Because of our double minority status as Black women living in a society in which racism, discrimination, sexism, and gender role expectations are alive and well, we have legitimate reasons not to trust—ourselves and others. Early in life, many of us were spoon-fed idioms such as "Little girls should be seen and not heard." We were taught to make ourselves small, disregard our feelings, and keep our opinions to ourselves. And when we did dare speak up, we were often met with invalidation—told directly or indirectly that our thoughts and feelings are irrelevant or irrational. Though there are exceptions, over time, these experiences of being censored and receiving negative feedback can teach us not to trust ourselves. Lack of self-trust often manifests as constantly second-guessing the choices we make, questioning whether our thoughts or feelings are valid, ignoring or discounting our intuition and constantly seeking reassurance from others, and simply avoiding making decisions altogether. Domestic violence can exacerbate our challenges with self-trust.

The cultural pressures we face as Black women can also affect our level of trust in ourselves and others. Within the Black community, women experience intense pressure to be "superwomen," as we are often the cornerstone of the Black community. We are expected to be strong, self-sacrificing, and display no emotional distress in the face of daily life stress. Trained up from an early age, we become skilled at putting on a happy face, hiding our struggles and vulnerabilities, suppressing our emotions, and neglecting our own needs to help and protect others. This can negatively affect trust, by disconnecting us from our own emotional experiences and causing us to discount or ignore warning signals that something is wrong internally or in an unhealthy relationship.

The legacy of racism, police brutality, and unjust legal practices in America has taught some of us that it's not safe to trust the police, many of whom are members of majority groups. When dealing with domestic violence, you, as a Black woman, are put in the position of having to choose between your own safety and the safety of the Black man who abused you. Rather than reporting abuse to the authorities and receiving the resources and support you deserve, Black women who suffer abuse at the hands of a Black man are expected to "take one for the team," to save Black men from unfair treatment by a prejudiced legal system.

On top of all of this, stereotypes that portray Black women as overly sexual, bossy, headstrong, and undermining to Black men lead us to be blamed when we come forward with disclosures of domestic violence. The generational cycle of abuse can negatively impact trust. Survivors who come from families where their mothers and grandmothers experienced domestic violence, when they reach out for support from family members who are also survivors, may be met with apathy or scolding for not being strong enough to handle the abuse. These negative experiences or fear of these experiences can cause you to not take the risk of trusting others, choosing instead to hide your pain. When you hide your pain, you are more vulnerable to continued abuse, and you are less likely to receive the emotional and social supports and services you deserve.

Within the Black community, faith and spirituality play a major role in helping members cope with the stressors they face in daily life. Black women in the midst of domestic violence are highly likely to seek support from a pastor or trusted member of their religious organization. Unfortunately, it's not uncommon for Black women to be subtly blamed for the abuse they experience, or to be encouraged to "stick it out" in an abusive relationship by religious leaders. If you have had this experience, it can cause you to blame yourself for the abuse, or to lose faith that if you reach out for support you will receive the help you need.

Similarly, if you have a history of abuse or neglect from other Black family members or members of the Black community, this may have caused you to develop negative beliefs about the Black community as a whole, and you may find it difficult to trust another Black person— even helping professionals such as therapists, social workers, or community leaders, who could help support you in exiting and healing from an abusive relationship.

Learning to Trust Yourself

We have covered several reasons why Black women domestic violence survivors may have trust difficulties. Now we'd like to turn our attention to how you can learn how to trust yourself and others. We'll start with self-trust.

Learning to trust yourself begins with getting to know yourself. Why? Because it's hard to have faith in someone you barely know. According to marriage researcher and therapist John Gottman, *attunement* is a process for building trust in romantic relationships. Attunement can be thought of as our ability to recognize and be with expression of emotion; it's traditionally thought of as something that happens between two people. For example, if I walk in a room and a loved one is crying, I am attuned to them if I notice their tears, express that I am moved by seeing their tears, ask why they are crying, actively listen to their answer, and respond supportively. Lack of attunement would look like me not even noticing that they were crying, ignoring their tears, or harshly criticizing them for "being too sensitive." Although Gottman's theory of attunement developed out of research with couples, we believe it can be an incredibly rich way of building self-trust.

Journal Prompts

We encourage you to grab your journal. Please pause, reflect, and respond to the following prompts authentically. This is an opportunity for you to connect what you've been reading to your own life.

1. When you are in emotional pain (e.g., feeling sadness, shame, grief, rage, or disappointment), how do you respond?

2. How often are you there for yourself in a kind and understanding way?

3. How attuned would you consider yourself to be to your own emotional suffering?

If you consider yourself to be less attuned, you might benefit from developing the skill of attunement. For many survivors, learning to trust themselves is new and may even be scary. The good news about attunement is it's a skill that can be developed, much like learning how to swim, cook, or ride a bike. The more you practice the skill of attunement or "tuning inward" to yourself, the more you will increase the habit of attunement and the more you will begin to trust yourself.

The Six Ingredients of Attunement

There are six ingredients to attunement: awareness, turning toward, tolerance, understanding, non-defensive responding, and empathy. Let's explore each and discuss how you can practice each aspect of attunement to increase self-trust.

1. Awareness

Awareness involves checking in with yourself periodically. It can look like checking your "emotional temperature" by asking yourself questions like: "How am I doing?" "What am I feeling today?" "What emotion best describes my current mood?" As a starting point, it can be helpful to take your emotional temperature twice a day—once in the morning when you wake up, and once before you go to bed at night. Awareness also involves knowing your thoughts, habits, values, morals, and needs.

Questions you can ask yourself to gain greater self-awareness include: "What do I need the most (emotionally, physically, socially, etc.) today?" "When do I feel most vulnerable?" "What makes me uncomfortable?" "What is the most important thing in my life?" "What makes me happy?" "What makes me sad?" "What do I say to myself when I make mistakes?" "What type of person do I want to be?" "What are my strengths?" "What are my areas for improvement?" Self-awareness questions can be great to ask yourself when you notice you are feeling overwhelmed, stressed, or confused.

In addition to asking these questions, awareness involves accepting the response, whether it's positive or negative. As Black women, we often find ourselves in spaces where we have to mute certain aspects of ourselves, to fit in and make other people comfortable. Over time, perpetually muting ourselves can cause us to be disconnected from ourselves. The goal of increasing self-awareness is to know yourself better. This is important, because it can be easy to lose yourself and blindly take on other people's viewpoints, goals, and agenda. When you know yourself, you feel more confident expressing and advocating for yourself. Consistently speaking your truth and asking for what you need helps to build self-trust.

2. Turning Toward

The second aspect of attunement is *turning toward*. Turning toward involves a willingness to "be with" and "stay with" what you are feeling emotionally. When we are feeling emotional pain, it's natural to want to make it go away, ignore it, or try to change the emotion in some way. When we turn toward our emotion, we tell ourselves, "It's okay for you to feel what you are feeling. I am in this with you. I will not turn away from your pain or criticize you for feeling the way you feel."

Start practicing the skill of "turning toward" by labeling the specific emotion you are experiencing the next time you have an uncomfortable emotion, like sadness, grief, rage, anger, disappointment, fear, or frustration. After you have labeled the emotion, see if you can lovingly turn toward the emotion, softening your heart toward that emotion and allowing it to be as it is, without trying to make it different. This level of acceptance helps build familiarity with painful emotions and lets you know that you can experience difficult emotions without falling apart.

3. Tolerance

Tolerance involves seeing your thoughts, actions, perspectives, and emotions as acceptable and worthy of expressing, even when they differ from the viewpoints of others. A major part of tolerance is being willing to sit with the discomfort of expressing a viewpoint that differs from others'; this can be especially difficult for people-pleasers, who draw self-worth from the approval of others and are hesitant to disagree with others for fear of being disapproved of.

One concrete way to work on building tolerance for the discomfort that comes with holding a different perspective is experience. Be on the lookout for times you are presented with ideas or perspectives that you don't agree with. Instead of remaining silent, challenge yourself to speak up. Your voice may shake at the beginning, but with continued practice speaking up, you will grow more comfortable. Remember, disagreeing is not a personal attack on the person you disagree with; it's a way of avoiding future resentment and frustration. Your perspective is just as valuable as anyone else's.

Another key aspect of tolerance is being willing to experience the discomfort that naturally comes with making decisions. When we don't trust ourselves, the tendency is to procrastinate and not make any decisions, for fear that we will make the wrong decision. Or we constantly seek other people's opinions about what decision we should make. Getting feedback and advice from trusted others is not bad—it only becomes problematic when we rely too heavily on others for decision making, or get in the habit of viewing other people's opinion as more important and valid than our own. The only way we will come to trust ourselves is by taking decisive action and learning from the decisions we make, whether those decisions turn out to be good or bad. Also, when you make a decision, stick with it. Constantly second-guessing or questioning your decisions makes trusting yourself even more challenging.

Related to making decisions is pursuing goals. When we don't trust ourselves, we may not pursue goals like going back to school, starting a business, or dating again, either because we don't trust ourselves to follow through or because we have experienced failure in this area in the past. Building self-trust includes being willing to tolerate the discomfort of pursuing your goals, when there is no guarantee that you will reach them.

To set yourself up for success, break big goals down into smaller steps. For example, if my goal is to go back to school, I might break that goal down into the following steps: 1. Research colleges in my area. 2. Decide on one or two degrees I am interested in pursuing. 3. Compile a list of application materials and deadlines. 4. Complete application materials. 5. Request letters of recommendation. 6. Submit my application.

Breaking my larger goal down into small, manageable chunks makes the goal seem less daunting and increases the chances that I will actually reach my ultimate goal. Experiencing success with one goal increases confidence to pursue other more challenging goals.

4. Understanding

Understanding involves seeking to know the factors that contribute to your emotions, perspectives, and behaviors. An important part of understanding is digging beneath the surface of your preferences, values, and triggers to understand their origins. For example, say you are sitting at a restaurant with someone you are newly dating, and you share a fear you have. Wanting to comfort you, the person reaches out and gently touches your hand. The act of touching your hand triggers feelings of unsafety and defensiveness. As a result, you abruptly snatch back your hand and get up and go to the restroom.

Understanding, in this situation, might look like taking a deep breath and exploring what about the touching of your hand triggered the uneasy feelings. You might discover that the way your hand was touched was similar to the way an abusive partner used to touch your hand. This additional information makes it *understandable* that you reacted the way you did. Rather than leaving the situation confused, having this understanding gives you the clarity needed to explain your experience to the person. It also positions you to ask for what you need in similar situations in the future.

5. Non-defensive Responding

Non-defensive responding is exactly what it sounds like. It involves pausing long enough to respectfully listen to what your body needs and wants (especially when you are in emotional or physical pain), while withholding judgment and negative self-talk.

Let's revisit the example of a new dating partner triggering feelings of unsafety and defensiveness by touching your hand in a way that reminds you of an abusive partner. Non-defensive responding might look like paying attention to the feelings in your body that let you know you feel unsafe: maybe a sinking feeling in your stomach, tightness in your chest, or sudden sensations of heat in your face. You might find that, instead of abruptly leaving the situation, you are able to verbalize the discomfort you are experiencing and ask for a different method of comforting, such as gentle, reassuring words. You might even be able to say, "I noticed that when you touched my hand I felt a wave of heat flash through my body. This lets me know that I don't feel safe being touched in this way. I am working on growing more comfortable with physical touch, but for now, reassuring words are my preferred way of being comforted by you."

Defensive responding would probably result in a defensive response, where you reject, ignore, "push through," suppress, or scold yourself for feeling the way you feel. This type of dismissing or disapproval of your own feelings impacts self-trust, because it teaches you that your feelings are wrong and not worthy of your attention.

6. Empathy

The last part of attunement is *empathy*. Empathy involves communicating to yourself in a kind and compassionate manner. This is critically important when you have fallen short of your expectations of yourself, experience a failure, or are disappointed in yourself. Rather than being overly harsh or critical, you would try to talk to yourself the way that you would talk to a small child who is learning to walk and has just stumbled. Rather than judge them for falling, you would be gentle, encourage the child to get back up, reassure them that you believe in them, and let them know that no matter how many times they fall, you will be there for them. This is the same type of relationship we are encouraging you to build with yourself.

Learning to trust yourself will be a process. It will not happen overnight, and it will not be linear—you will not be perfect at trusting yourself, and you will face setbacks, challenges, and downward spirals. But there will also be moments of recovery and steady progress. The goal is to keep making small steps toward trusting yourself, despite the difficulties and discomfort you experience along the way. Remember, trust is built in small steps, slowly, over time.

Learning to Trust Others

"Trust is built in very small moments… In any given interaction, there is a possibility of connecting…or turning away… [I]f you're always choosing to turn away, then trust erodes in a relationship— very gradually, very slowly."

—John Gottman

Now we will shift our attention toward learning how to trust others. As we've previously discussed, you probably have many very valid reasons for not trusting people. The fact that you were violated, harmed, or betrayed by a person who was supposed to love, respect, and nurture you is evidence that people are not always who they say they are and they don't always behave in the way that we expect them to. In the aftermath of domestic violence, many survivors give themselves a hard time for not "seeing the abuse coming" or for ignoring early warning signs. They begin to question their judgment and conclude that they are unable to tell whom they can or cannot trust. It seems easier, and safer, to assume the worst about everyone and trust no one.

The problem with this approach is that, if you have left the abusive relationship, it's not informed by the current, nontraumatic conditions. Not trusting anyone is safe, maybe even necessary, when you are in a traumatic environment and vulnerable to being taken advantage of.

However, in non-abusive relationships with a safe friend, partner, or family member, rigidly applying the "trust no one" rule is going to make it nearly impossible to enjoy a healthy, happy, and close relationship with anyone. No one wants to have to continuously prove themselves trustworthy over and over again, only to have their trustworthy behaviors be ignored and met with skepticism. And on your end, it's exhausting to constantly be on guard with everyone all the time.

We want to support you in beginning the process of learning how to trust others. A starting point is shifting your mindset about trust. Many of us approach trust as black or white, but it's not that simple. There are different types of trust and trust falls on a continuum.

It's rare to trust everybody in our lives completely, a term for which is *global trust*. What's more common is partial trust—where we trust certain people with certain things. Let's say you have a coworker named Leisha. You've worked with Leisha for two months. Although you've only had small talk with Leisha about her weekend activities and the weather, she has always been friendly to you; she shows up to work every day and seems committed to performing her job well, and generally has a good attitude when you run into her. Based on your limited knowledge of Leisha, it might be reasonable to assume that you would trust her to be a team member on a new work project you've been tasked with leading. However, you probably wouldn't trust her with your deepest secret or the keys to your home. On the other hand, you might trust your best friend, Kerri, with your secrets and the keys to your home. The same goes for everyone else in your life, even acquaintances and strangers—we trust some people with some things, but it's not healthy or safe to trust everyone with everything.

So, when it comes to trust, it's not a black-and-white matter of, Do you trust people: yes or no? The better question is: How much do you trust a particular person? With what information? Under what circumstances?

For survivors who think they have a long way to go with trust because they don't trust anyone, we challenge you to reconsider. We all place our trust in someone or something every day, sometimes with little awareness that we are trusting. This goes for the Internet connection in your home, your banking organization, postal service workers, restaurant waiters, and church members. You trust that when you tap your favorite app on your phone, it will give you the content you want to see. We trust our banks or credit unions to protect the money we've entrusted to them. We place trust in postal service workers to deliver packages to our door in one piece. We trust restaurant workers to exercise cleanliness with handling our food and beverages, and our church members to give us support.

The good news about these little daily trust decisions is that you can build on them, to learn how to grow your ability to trust the people you want to be in healthy, trusting relationships with—whether it's a family member, romantic partner, work associate, or friend.

Here are some practical strategies for learning to trust others.

Know Your Unhelpful Assumptions and Patterns

As we have described, awareness is the breeding ground for change. Once you are aware of the specific challenges you face with trust, you will be in a better position to do something about them. In the aftermath of trauma, to keep yourself safe, you may have developed certain rules (e.g., trust no one under any circumstances) or thinking patterns ("If I trust someone, then I will be hurt"). Although these rules and ways of thinking helped to keep you safe in abusive environments, they are not so effective in relationships where abuse is not occurring. You may be unaware of these patterns, because they are automatic and operate on an unconscious level.

To move toward your goal of learning how to trust others, it's important to understand how your experience with domestic violence impacted trust. This will look different for each individual survivor.

Journal Prompts

These journal prompts can help you discover the impact that domestic violence has had on your behaviors, thoughts, and feelings when it comes to trusting others. Please take out your journal and write authentic, unfiltered responses to each.

1. When you meet someone new, what assumptions do you make about their trustworthiness? What are these assumptions based on?

2. Do you believe it's possible for you to find a partner who is faithful, respectful, and loving toward you? Why or why not?

3. Are there things you think are true about all potential partners, or the majority of them?

4. Do you believe that all potential partners are dangerous, aggressive, unfaithful, manipulative, or "wolves in sheep's clothing"?

5. How has your tendency toward trusting others changed since you experienced domestic violence?

6. Do you put people through "tests" to determine whether they can be trusted? After they demonstrate consistent trustworthy behavior, does your trust grow, or do you remain suspicious of them? Do people have to keep proving themselves over and over again before you will trust them?

Begin in the Middle: The Trust Continuum

Because trust is best thought of as a continuum, as opposed to black and white, consider the following:

Extreme Distrust	Neutral	Extreme Trust

Considering that you have been betrayed in the past, when deciding whether or not to trust someone you just met, you may start at the far left of the spectrum, with extreme distrust of everyone—even if you don't have any evidence that they are untrustworthy. This is a hard place for people who don't know you well to be placed because, in their view, it can seem like a never-ending battle to gain your trust. Starting everyone at the place of extreme distrust is like buying a brand-new appliance that requires AA batteries and trying to operate it with AAA batteries. Even though the appliance is new, it won't work if you use the wrong type of batteries. Similarly, when you enter into a new relationship with a person you are unfamiliar with, if you treat them as if they are extremely untrustworthy to begin with, a relationship with potential may never realize its full potential, because trust was never given an opportunity to grow.

If you want to be in healthy relationships with people, you must learn to give them an opportunity to build trust with you. Hear us clearly: We are NOT suggesting that you swing all the way to the right and start off each relationship with extreme trust. Rather, we are inviting you to consider what it might be like to begin in the middle, with neutral trust.

When you begin in the middle, you are open to letting new information in from the current relationship, rather than holding a new person responsible for the hurt and the pain that was inflicted by someone else. Here is an example of how this might play out: Suppose you text a new romantic interest during a time when you are certain they are available to text back. It takes five hours for them to text you back. They apologize for taking so long to text back and inform you that they were asleep when your text came through.

In this situation, because of your desire to protect yourself from betrayal, it could be second nature to be extremely distrusting and assume that they are spending time with someone else, and begin distancing yourself from the relationship. However, if you take a moment to breathe after the text message reply comes through, and approach this situation from a neutral standing, you can move the person right or left on the trust continuum, based on your experience with them.

To take this idea further, you can draw a different line for specific types of trust. For example, line A might represent "trust them to borrow money," line B "trust them with a secret," line C "trust them to be reliable and do what they say they will do," and line D "trust them to communicate effectively, even when we disagree about a certain topic." When you begin in the middle, you free yourself from having to make quick, global trust judgments that might turn out to be wrong. By beginning in the middle, you allow a person to earn trust in a variety of areas over time.

Each new person you encounter can start with four dots (one for each type of trust) in the middle of each trust line. Based on your experiences with the person, each type of trust will either move farther to the left or farther to the right, indicating growths or declines in trust.

You can think of it like students in elementary school. At the beginning of the school year, each student starts with a blank slate, and they earn points based on their academic performance. Some students excel in all subjects, while others excel in some subjects but struggle with other subjects.

In the same way, it's possible that some people will grow in some trust areas but decline in others. If this happens, it doesn't necessarily mean that you can't have a relationship with them. Rather, this information can show you the type of boundaries you need to set in the relationship. For example, you could choose to trust someone to pay back a $100 loan, but not trust them with a secret.

Let Experience Be Your Teacher

The definition of learning is "to gain knowledge of or skill in through study, instruction, or experience." When you are learning to trust someone, you do just that—gain knowledge of their trustworthiness by studying their actions and noticing your experiences of them, in addition to how others have experienced them. In this way, you allow your learning to be the deciding factor in whether or not you should trust them.

One way to approach your information-gathering is like a scientist. Psychologist Aphrodite Matsakis has outlined a helpful five-step approach for assessing trustworthiness, which we recommend trying out.

1. **Gather information.** Pay attention to what you have seen, heard, and experienced around or about the person you are wanting to trust. This will require you to spend time around the person, or even to get the "411" on them from mutual friends. If you are venturing into dating, it might also be important to gather information about what their relationship with their ex is like and/or how it ended.

2. **Form an opinion.** Based on the information you have gathered about this person over time, form a "best guess" about their trustworthiness. Remember, instead of making global judgments about their trustworthiness, we recommend you focus on a specific type of trust that you are trying to develop with them (e.g., trust with money, trust with your heart, trust being alone with them).

3. **Look for Evidence to Support Your Opinion.** Put on your scientist hat. Assuming the information you are gathering points in the direction of the person being trustworthy, continue engaging with them (in a way that feels safe and comfortable for you). Remain open to evidence that is in support of or contrary to your "best guess" from step two.

4. **Revisit your hypothesis.** Take stock of the additional information you have gathered. Does it seem to mostly confirm or disconfirm your "best guess"? If the evidence is contrary to your best guess, you may want to modify it. For example, if you were thinking that someone was "probably trustworthy" to go on a second date with, but during a recent phone conversation they became noticeably irritable and dismissive as you shared your boundaries around sex and intimacy, maybe you want to modify your best guess to "probably not trustworthy" or "neutral."

5. **Repeat as Necessary.** Building trust is a marathon, not a sprint. It will take time to know whether someone is

trustworthy. And because people can change, it's best to always be open to letting new information in. Think of building trust as a process that can take weeks, months, or even years. There doesn't need to be a goal of getting to the side of extreme trust. You are always learning, growing, and changing. The person you are in a relationship with is likely also growing, learning, and changing. Be open to this process.

Trust Your Gut

Pay attention to the "vibe" you get when you are around someone you're uncertain about trusting. There's a saying: "Trust your gut, she knows what's up." Depending on how you were raised, you might be more or less familiar with your gut feelings, or intuition, which will impact how comfortable you feel trusting them. Gut reactions can be thought of as internal indicator lights—similar to the check engine light in a car—that give us information. Since they can often be subtle, it's important to really tune in.

One way to do this is to pay attention to how you feel in your body when you're around a person, when you're anticipating interacting with them, or in the hours and days following an interaction with them. Places to tune in inside your body include your head, heart, stomach, shoulders, breath, and jaw. Is there any tension, knots, clenching, bracing, or discomfort present? What might be causing the tension?

The presence of activity in the body is not always a negative thing. For example, it's normal to feel butterflies in your stomach when you're nervous because you want to make a good impression on someone who you like. On the other hand, you can feel uneasiness in your stomach when you're scared or feel unsafe around someone. Because the difference is subtle, we might think it means one thing when really it means another. There are many different ways to interpret the same bodily reaction. Therefore, it will be important for you to get curious about what is motivating your "gut" reactions. This is where self-attunement comes back into play. Trust decisions are most powerful when they are informed by a combination of learning through experience *and* your gut reactions.

Closing Comments on Trust

One of the reasons why trust is so tricky is because we cannot read people's minds. Therefore, we can never predict someone else's actions with 100 percent accuracy. All we have is our best guess.

In many instances of domestic violence, the perpetrator initially behaves in ways that are trustworthy, even when they are not. When someone manipulates you in this way, it can become hard to trust yourself. Because perfection is an illusion and you're human, it's possible to make trust decisions that you later come to realize were wrong. No one gets it right all the time.

Along this journey of learning how to trust yourself and others, it's imperative that you give yourself grace. At any given moment, you make the best decision you have with the information (knowledge and gut instinct) you have available to you at the time. This is really all we can expect of ourselves.

Hindsight is always 20/20. We encourage you to refrain from judging past decisions based on information that was not available to you in that moment. Other times, you may ignore the information that was available to you, or ignore your gut feeling. Again, you're human. Don't fall into the trap of expecting perfection from yourself. Often, the best approach is viewing your past trust decisions as lessons that can be applied as you move forward in your recovery from domestic violence.

Support from safe family members, friends, and trained professionals can be very helpful in learning how to trust again. As you're learning to trust yourself and others, it's helpful to surround yourself with people who give wise advice, don't excuse or tolerate violence, and who encourage and respect your decision-making. Mental health professionals can be an awesome source of support to Black women who are learning to trust again. Because trust was broken in a relationship, it can be best repaired in a relationship. In working with a mental health professional, you get to experience the qualities of a healthy, trusting relationship, and this relationship can serve as a powerful model that you can structure other relationships around.

Journal Prompts

1. How have my notions of trust been impacted by the domestic violence I experienced?

2. Reflect on your past relationships. What specific gut reactions have indicated that a person is trustworthy?

3. What gut reactions have indicated that a person is untrustworthy?

4. How have you responded to those gut reactions, and how would you like to?

5. Who is a safe support person that you can rely on to encourage you along your journey of learning to trust yourself and others?

CHAPTER 6

Cultivating Self-Esteem and Self-Worth

I need to see my own beauty and to continue to be reminded that I am enough, that I am worthy of love without effort, that I am beautiful, that the texture of my hair and that the shape of my curves, the size of my lips, the color of my skin, and the feelings that I have are all worthy and okay.

—Tracee Ellis Ross

Self-esteem is your view of yourself as likable, worthy, capable, and valuable. A good indicator of self-esteem is the way you talk to yourself. If someone could be a fly on the wall of your mind, what kind of self-talk would they hear? Constantly putting yourself down and thinking thoughts like "I am damaged; I am ugly; I am worthless and incapable" are indicators of low self-esteem. On the other hand, thoughts like "I am worthy of love and happiness; I can accomplish my goals; I attract good things into my life; My past does not define me" are signs of high self-esteem. Your self-esteem is influenced by your self-assessment of yourself, the people you compare yourself with, and the way other people treat you.

As a Black woman who is vulnerable to racism and sexism, common everyday experiences likely challenge your self-esteem. For Black women, having high self-esteem is an uphill climb. Our society has a plethora of negative images of Black women that are constantly regurgitated. Black women are portrayed as domineering, sexually promiscuous, lazy, and uneducated. These stereotypes can make it difficult to have high self-esteem as a Black woman. Additionally, beauty standards in American society privilege light skin and European hair, eye color, and facial features.

These preferences shape the way Black women are viewed in society, influence opportunities for career and economic advancement, impact how frequently Black women have rewarding experiences or supportive relationships, and affect the overall way Black women see themselves. In sum, when you grow up as a Black woman in a society where "White is right," it will impact your sense of self. Self-esteem is impacted by both inner critical messages and external oppressive forces, which only make the inner critical messages louder.

Domestic violence can be especially damaging to self-esteem. You may have recognized some differences in the way you viewed yourself before you experienced domestic violence, compared to the way you viewed yourself after you experienced domestic violence. It's very common for survivors to believe they are "damaged goods" or "unworthy of love" because of the abuse they experienced. Survivors who blame themselves for the violence they experienced, and those who cope by avoiding everything they fear, have lower self-esteem.

If you have internalized societal myths that portray Black women as sexually promiscuous, difficult, or combative, this could erode your self-esteem and lead you to believe that you're to blame for the abuse. We want to assure you that these societal myths are *wrong* and you're *not* to blame for the abuse you experienced. After breaking free from an abusive partner, in hindsight, many women ask "How could I have been so stupid?" This is not about you being stupid. The tactics of abuse are *designed* to make you question yourself, but the only person who deserves judgment and blame is the abuser. Self-judgment and condemnation are not the answer. Cultivating self-esteem and self-worth will help you to be less judgmental of yourself.

There are five practices you can use to reclaim your self-esteem: become aware of your thoughts and self-talk; remember that not everything you think is true; replace overly critical thoughts and self-talk; take back your power; and surround yourself with people who think highly of themselves and you.

Be Aware of Your Thoughts and Self-Talk

There is a saying that goes: *Watch your thoughts; they become words. Watch your words; they become actions. Watch your actions; they become habits. Watch your habits; they become character. Watch your character; it becomes your destiny.* No truer words have ever been spoken when it comes to self-esteem.

Black women are constantly bombarded with stigmatizing messages that they are too domineering, emasculating, and overly sexual, and therefore, are deserving of abuse or somehow to blame for any violence they experience. What's worse, when they come forward with abuse allegations, Black women are often met with skepticism, little sympathy, and speculation about what they did to "deserve" such treatment. You may have had the experience of telling someone about your situation and not being taken seriously, or having the other person try to justify the abuse. After repeatedly facing this speculation and hearing these stigmatizing messages, they can become so internalized that you start seeing yourself through the lens of these harmful false stereotypes. The best way to begin to deprogram yourself is to be aware of what your thoughts are saying.

Notice Your Thoughts

A first step to improving your self-esteem is to become aware of your thoughts about yourself and the words you speak to yourself. Awareness is key, because we cannot change or heal what we refuse to acknowledge. Once you become aware of how you're thinking about and talking to yourself, you can take steps to make positive changes that support your self-esteem. Keep in mind, the process of becoming more aware is not an open invitation to judge yourself. It's simply about noticing what thoughts you have, so you can decide how you want to respond.

Approach the noticing with curiosity and kindness. The way you think about and speak to yourself was more than likely impacted by the domestic violence you endured. Here are a few questions to help you connect with how you think about yourself. Make sure you have your journal and a pen ready to help you reflect.

Journal Prompts

1. Has domestic violence affected the way you think about yourself or how you take care of yourself?

2. Since the domestic violence ended, when someone gives you a compliment, how does it make you feel?

3. Do you believe you deserve to be happy?

4. List your three greatest strengths.

5. List your three greatest weaknesses.

6. When you make a mistake, don't live up to your expectations, or don't reach your goals, what do you say to yourself?

Look back over your responses to these questions. Circle the thoughts that are destructive or harmful to your self-esteem. If you have trouble determining whether a thought is destructive or not, ask yourself: "Would I say this to or about a close friend?" If the answer is "no," it's more than likely a negative thought. Another way to know whether a thought is negative or unhelpful is to see if it falls into any of the following categories:

- *Jumping to conclusions:* Reaching a negative conclusion with few to no facts. For example, "I'm forty-five and still single. I guess I'll just be single for the rest of my life."

- *Exaggerating:* Making things bigger or more intense than what they really are. For example, "Every time I open my mouth, I say something stupid. I am worthless."

- *Disregarding context:* Overlooking important factors that influence behavior. For example, "I should have known better than to choose an abusive partner."

- *Minimizing:* Discounting your feelings, strengths, actions, and impact. For example, "My feelings were hurt when she cursed at me, but I'm probably just being too sensitive."

- *Oversimplifying:* Making things simpler than what they are, or making things all good/bad or all right/wrong. For example, "I allowed myself to be disrespected in my last relationship and didn't do anything to stop it. I'm pathetic."

- *Overgeneralizing:* Taking a single negative experience and applying it to all similar future experiences. For example, "The last person I dated hurt me. I can't be trusted to choose a good partner."

- *Mind-reading:* Assuming you know what other people are thinking about you. For example, "She looked at me weird, so she must not like me."

- *Emotional reasoning:* Taking your feelings as facts. For example, "I don't feel worthy of love, so I must be unlovable."

To increase your awareness of how often you think or speak destructively to yourself, here's an exercise you can try. Get a rubber band, simple bracelet, or hair tie and place it around one of your wrists. When you notice yourself thinking something that is destructive to your self-esteem, simply switch the rubber band, bracelet, or hair tie to your opposite wrist. Practice this for three days over the next week and notice how often you're needing to change wrists.

Question Your Thoughts

Actor and comedian Emo Philips once said, "I used to think the brain was the most wonderful organ in my body. Then I realized who was telling me this." As this quote illustrates, our brain can tell us things that are not true. Instead of automatically assuming that every thought we think about ourselves is true, we can take a step back and acknowledge our thoughts for what they are: a temporary experience that may or may not be true. Taking this step back is a helpful strategy, because the thoughts we have about ourselves can be incredibly painful.

To reduce the pain you feel as a result of destructive thoughts, remind yourself that every thought you have about yourself is not necessarily a fact. Try this practice: The next time you have an unhelpful thought that is destructive to your self-esteem, acknowledge the thought by saying to yourself: "I'm having the thought that I'm _____."

For example, if the unhelpful, self-esteem-eroding thought you have is "I'm worthless," first, say the thought to yourself as it originally came to you: "I'm worthless." Notice how it feels to think this about yourself.

Next, say to yourself, "I'm having the thought that I'm worthless." Notice the difference in how you feel.

Lastly, say to yourself, "I'm noticing that I'm having the thought that I'm worthless." Take a moment to notice how you feel now.

By taking you from being the unhelpful thought, to having the thought, to noticing the thought, this simple practice creates space between you and your thoughts, so that you can be reminded that this thought is simply content your brain is giving you that is not necessarily true. This frees you up to simply observe the self-esteem-eroding thought rather than getting caught up in it. When you observe your thoughts, you can work skillfully with them.

Replace Critical Thoughts

Now that you have identified the unhelpful, self-esteem-eroding thoughts, it's important to come up with more positive ways of thinking about and talking to yourself. This is critical because the longer you allow these thoughts to stay in your brain unchecked, the further they will continue to erode your self-esteem. There is a Bible verse that reads:

> "Death and life are in the power of the tongue, and those who love it will eat its fruits."

> —Proverbs 18:21 ESV

Sometimes we take our words for granted. Allow this verse to serve as a reminder that your words have power—even the words that stay in your head and are never spoken aloud. The most immediate impact of our words is that they impact how we feel and the way we behave toward ourselves and others. Consistently thinking things like: "I'm unlovable," "I don't deserve to be happy," "I'm damaged," and "I don't measure up" will make you feel terrible about yourself, and these thoughts will not help motivate you to take the actions necessary to heal from the domestic violence you experienced—just the opposite.

What words have you been saying to yourself in your mind? Are the words you say to and think about yourself life-giving or destructive? Does your self-talk make you feel important, affirmed, and motivated to heal? If your self-talk could use a bit of makeover, here's how to do it.

Journal Prompts

Grab your journal. Write down each destructive thought you have identified so far while reading this chapter.

Go through each thought one by one and ask yourself, "What would be a more compassionate and self-affirming thing to say to myself?" Beneath each original thought, write the alternate thought. For example, if you think, "I'm unworthy," instead you can say to yourself, "Even though I sometimes feel like I have no worth, when I pause and reflect, I can identify areas in my life where I make valuable contributions."

The idea is to develop an alternative thought that is kind and nurtures your self-esteem. If you have trouble developing an alternative statement, it can be helpful to think about what you would tell a dear friend or small child in your community who was thinking the original thought about themselves. You might also draw on the wisdom of an ancestor you admire and consider how they would respond to the original thought.

As a Black woman, in addition to the common challenges of womanhood, you will more than likely face racism and oppression. Racism and racial discrimination can negatively impact your mental health, resulting in stress, depression, and poor physical health. The way you talk to yourself in the face of this race-based stress will help you to navigate these negative experiences while also protecting your overall health and wellness. Practicing positive, affirming self-talk in daily life can also be a buffer for your self-esteem. The higher your self-esteem is, the less negatively your mental health will be impacted by racism and discrimination.

It's important to note that the intention of coming up with more self-compassionate things to say to yourself is not intended to dismiss, minimize, or negate your current feelings about yourself. Every thought and feeling you have comes from a real place, whether it was influenced by your past relationship or some other experience. Some of our thoughts have developed over time or served as coping strategies to protect us from future hurt or pain. We might have grown up in homes where negative talk was used as a form of "tough love," to motivate us or give us tougher skin to face the various challenges in the world. Or maybe choosing to accept thoughts like "I'm unlovable" as truth makes the pain of not being in a relationship more bearable. If you train yourself to believe you're unworthy or undeserving of your heart's deepest desires, it hurts less when you don't receive them.

Although this way of thinking or coping may have helped you survive, it's not a healthy strategy for the long-term. But when developing more compassionate thoughts, we don't want to completely dismiss your self-esteem-eroding thoughts. They have served a purpose for you in the past by making your pain more manageable, and that is important to acknowledge. The spirit of this practice we're suggesting is to look at how useful or helpful the destructive thoughts are to you right now. If a thought is not useful, it's important to modify it so it can become more useful to you.

Claim Your Power

As we have learned, domestic violence is largely about power and control. As a survivor of domestic violence, you had a lot of power taken away from you against your will. Now that you're no longer in a violent intimate relationship, there are ways that you can practice taking back your power. Developing your self-esteem builds toward feeling entitled to take up space and advocate for your needs and wants.

Here are some practical ways you can experiment with taking back your power. Each of these skills requires practice and courage when your self-worth has been damaged or destroyed by domestic violence. Be gentle and patient with yourself as you begin practicing taking back your power.

- **Ask for what you need or want.** Think about the relationships you're involved in, whether they be with family, friends, coworkers, community members, or non-abusive partners. Consider areas where your needs are not being met and how you could ask for what you need or want.

- **Set boundaries in your relationships.** Boundaries can run the gamut from letting an acquaintance know the types of information you feel comfortable sharing with them, making a request for someone standing too close for comfort to respect your personal bubble in public, identfying topics of conversation that are "off limits" with friends (e.g., diet or body-shaming talk), or asking someone to stop cracking jokes that you find offensive.

- **Reclaim time for self-care.** Self-care is all about nurturing your body, soul, and mind, so that you have the energy and clarity needed to thrive in life. It involves doing pleasurable things you enjoy, as well as the not-so-pleasant things that are good for your health (e.g., regular dental and medical check-ups, saying no to additional tasks when your plate is overflowing, and walking away from relationships that have run their course). We will spend more time on various types of self-care in chapter 10.

- **Be honest with yourself and others about what you think and feel.** You can practice this by noticing your tendency to "go with the flow" in group situations and challenging yourself to speak your truth, even if others might disagree. In the long run, you build confidence when you don't betray yourself by denying or hiding your true thoughts or feelings.

- **Recognize that you have the power to choose how you will respond.** When you're feeling afraid, upset, or stuck in your life, you can decide how you will respond to the situation. When angry, frustrated, or sad, it can feel as though your actions are outside of your control. No matter how unpleasant the situation, you always have a choice in how you respond.

- **Prioritize what matters most to you.** Allow your values to guide how and where you spend your time and energy. Each of us only has twenty-four hours every day. We can't do "all the things" without eventually running ourselves into the ground or neglecting our self-care. For certain seasons in life, some activities must take the back burner. Staying in contact with your values will help you to prioritize what matters most.

- **Take active steps to heal—mentally, emotionally, and spiritually.** Examples of this include reading this book or seeking therapy with a mental health professional.

Keep Good People Close

As you walk through your healing journey, it's important to have support. A sense of connection and community is foundational in Black culture and provides the optimal environment for healing. Healing from domestic violence can be enriched by family, friends, therapists, and community members who have high views of themselves and want the best for you. When you surround yourself with people who see the best in you even when you can't see it for yourself, you can more easily see yourself through their eyes.

Taking actions that reflect high self-esteem can feel challenging. Spending time with individuals who have high self-esteem can serve as a model for how you can begin taking actions that boost your self-esteem—simply surrounding yourself with supportive Black women who have pride, respect, and a positive outlook on life. This is because our self-evaluations are shaped by who we surround ourselves with. When we can see ourselves reflected in the people we admire, it affirms our worth, provides a sense of pride in being a Black woman, and shapes the way we view ourselves. If you find yourself feeling isolated, a good place to begin to build community might be Facebook groups, community groups based on a common interest or value, and local faith-based groups.

Related to the idea of community and connecting with others is religion, which could have a positive effect on self-esteem. Religion is thought to positively affect self-esteem, through teachings about the inherent value and worth of unconditional love. If you identify as a religious person or believe in a Higher Power who sees you as inherently valuable, worthy, and capable, it can boost your self-esteem to plug into your faith on a regular basis. This could be through prayer, reading a religious text, listening to spiritual songs, or connecting with a faith community.

Journal Prompts

1. If your self-esteem was as high as it could be, what thoughts would you have? What specific things would you say to yourself? How would you behave differently?

2. Pick one way to practice taking back your power over the next week (e.g., setting a boundary, asking for what you need, making a decision you've been putting off, etc.). Write it down in your journal. What challenges do you anticipate? How might you overcome those challenges?

3. Whom do you admire for their self-esteem and self-worth? What actions have you seen that person take that demonstrate a high regard for themselves? How can you emulate these actions in your own life?

CHAPTER 7

Letting Go of Guilt and Shame

You may not control all the events that happen to you, but you can decide not to be reduced by them.

—Maya Angelou

After a long time of rarely seeing each other, Zara and two of her closest girlfriends went out to their favorite restaurant to catch up. They had been close since they were young and considered each other more like family than friends. It had been hard for Zara to be away from their support and connection, but for the past couple of years she hadn't felt like she could share her life with them.

Zara had recently left a two-year abusive relationship, in which she was isolated and removed from her close relationships. For the first few months of the relationship, she and her partner, Blaine, spent time with her friends and saw them often. However, after some time, Zara saw them less and less. For Zara, part of her isolation was due to Blaine's insistence that they spend all their time together, without the distraction of other people; another part was Blaine's dislike of her friends.

Zara felt stuck between her friends and her relationship. She had no intention of letting go of her lifelong friends, but she also didn't want to let go of her new relationship. She tried to allow for more space between her and her friends, while also giving Blaine time to come around to the idea of them. Unfortunately, the space grew larger than Zara anticipated.

Once Blaine began to abuse her, Zara felt too humiliated to be around people. She felt guilty about letting her friendships slip away and embarrassed to have let them go for someone who was hurting her. It was especially upsetting once her friends began trying to support her in leaving—they knew some of what was going on in her relationship, because after all, they were like family to her. They knew enough to want her to end the relationship.

Zara felt ashamed of her situation and couldn't bear the thought of connecting with her friends and having to answer the question "How are things going with Blaine?" She kept picturing the conversation and could hear them asking "Why are you still there?" She didn't want to discuss that. Although she knew they had her best interests at heart, she couldn't shake the feeling that it seemed like they were questioning her, not just the relationship. Over time,

Zara stopped connecting with them. Before she knew it, more than a year had passed, and she had rarely seen or spoken with them.

They reconnected once Zara left the relationship. While Zara was happy to have dinner with them that evening, she also felt terrified of talking about her life for the past two years. She used to be worried about answering their questions about the relationship she was in, and now she was worried about answering questions about the relationship she had left. She blamed herself and was fearful about what her friends thought of her. She was anxious about the evening, but she also knew she needed it.

Journal Prompts

Take a moment and think about the thoughts and emotions Zara's story brings up for you. How is her story similar to or different from your own experiences? What would you say to Zara about the guilt, shame, and embarrassment that she felt? Is that message similar to or different from what you say to yourself? Journal about your responses and your overall thoughts.

Remember, being abused is never your fault. Is that reflected in what you wrote? You have been reading and processing the understanding that you didn't do anything to deserve being abused, you didn't do anything wrong to bring about the abuse, and you couldn't control someone else's behavior. You are not to blame for the abuse and manipulation that your partner inflicted on you.

Still, like Zara, you might feel a sense of guilt, shame, embarrassment, or other negative emotions that come with traumatic experiences. These emotions are natural, but they are also ones that most people want to change. Specifically, guilt and shame, which seem to linger longer than embarrassment, are emotions we will explore in this chapter. Without judging yourself for feeling any of these emotions, let's use this chapter to understand where they come from and what you can do about them.

The terms "guilt" and "shame" are often used together to describe how someone feels after they have reflected on a negative situation or experience. They are connected in ways that we will explore, but they are also different.

What Guilt Is

Guilt is feeling bad about something you did. It's connected to a specific action or set of actions that are perceived as being wrong, negative, or somehow worthy of blame. Perhaps you regret the action(s) and think you should have done something different. Maybe you would even say you should have done something "better." After all, you're unlikely to feel guilty if you think you did something good or in the right way. Instead, you likely feel guilty if you're negatively judging your behavior.

Notice that the focus here is about actions *you* have done. You should not feel guilty about the actions someone else has done. That guilt would be misplaced, because the action you perceived as being wrong, negative, or somehow worthy of blame is not yours to control. Think back to the understanding that being abused is never your fault, and you're not to blame for what your partner did. Feeling guilty over the abuse you endured would be misplaced, because your guilt would be about someone else's behavior.

Guilt implies some level of responsibility over the action that has occurred. Consider the statement "I feel guilty that a car was stolen." This statement implies that you stole the car. However, if your neighbor stole the car, then your guilt would seem strange. You would not say "I feel guilty that my neighbor stole a car." You may feel bad, saddened, disappointed, surprised, angry, or ambivalent, but guilt would not likely be the emotion that you would talk about.

The same applies to domestic violence. Guilt in this situation is misplaced, and unhelpful. Of course, domestic violence is not the same as a stolen car, but hopefully that example highlights that some things are out of your control and not your responsibility.

It's also important to acknowledge that some things are out of your control but may be partially your responsibility. Children witnessing domestic violence is an example of this. Your abusive partner may have engaged in physical violence in front of your children, or they may have used the children against you to exert power and control over you.

Even in this situation, the abuse is not your fault. The ownership still belongs to your abusive partner. You may feel the parenting aspect of shielding your children is your responsibility. That may be something you try to control, but it may be something that is not fully in your control in an abusive relationship. Perhaps you tried to shield your children, but the abuse you endured was too unpredictable to successfully do that. In this case, it would be important to evaluate what is in your control and how it connects to your guilt.

You might be surprised to learn that guilt connected to your own behavior has the potential to be helpful to you. Specifically, guilt can motivate change, if it's related to something you did or that you have responsibility for. For the guilt to be helpful, it must be connected to something that is in your control and that you can change.

Perhaps your relationship with your children changed throughout the course of the abusive relationship. Perhaps you feel guilty that you were less able to connect with them because of the abuse. Perhaps you feel guilty about how they have been (or could be) impacted by the abuse they witnessed. You can work, now, on being the parent you desire to be. You can work on supporting your children in their own healing journey. Guilt in these situations is specifically connected to things you can change, moving forward. Freeing yourself from abuse and working on your healing are important steps to help you through that.

Let's look at Zara's guilt, for another example. Zara stopped answering her friends' phone calls and messages. She stopped going places with them and doing the things that they used to do on a regular basis. Not answering phone calls and messages is an action that can be perceived in a negative way; Zara felt it was wrong. As she reflected on time she missed with her friends, she felt guilty for pulling back in their relationship. Zara can use her guilt as motivation to do something different and change her behavior. She can answer their phone calls and begin to repair the relationships. In this way, her guilt about the friendship is helpful to improving it.

Of course, guilt can only be motivating if it's not completely debilitating. That means you need to have enough guilt to inspire your change, but not so much guilt that you feel completely stuck in it. Consider the saying "She had a healthy amount of guilt." If the guilt feeling is too large, or is unresolved for too long, you run the risk of it turning into shame.

What Shame Is

Like guilt, shame is also a feeling connected to an action perceived as being wrong, negative, or somehow worthy of blame. Both guilt and shame are about thinking you did something bad. However, they differ: shame goes a step further and becomes about *who* you are, not just *what* you did. Shame becomes about you as a person. It can make you think you're a bad person because of bad actions. It can also lead you to think you're not deserving of good things, like love, connection, success, and more. The internalizing process of shame can lead to statements such as "I'm not worthy" or "I don't deserve _____."

Consider Zara, who felt a lot of concern about connecting with her friends. She felt guilty about her partner's actions of abusing her (misplaced guilt), and that guilt turned into shame. Zara felt too ashamed of her relationship, or her life, to be around others. Zara even felt she didn't deserve connection with her friends anymore. That thought represents internalized shame.

Shame is also connected to your moral, social, cultural, and spiritual compasses. These compasses are what guide your understanding of right and wrong. Naturally, your thoughts, feelings, and behaviors are likely led by what you consider to be morally acceptable, socially appropriate, culturally expected, or spiritually correct. In this way, shame is built from expectations and standards set by you, others close to you, and the larger systems of society.

The more you internalize and identify with your guiding expectations and standards of right and wrong, the more you will attribute violations of those standards to who you are. This is why shame leads you to think you're not deserving, or you're a bad person.

Let's take as an example the expectations society has on Black women and the messages of strength and resilience that come with them. If you value and adhere to the belief that you should be a Strong Black Woman, and you also see being abused as being weak, then you might feel shame over being abused. In this example, the action that occurred does not match an important and guiding part of your cultural expectations.

Likewise, if Zara values being a good friend and sees it as a part of her identity, when she does things she believes are socially inappropriate (e.g., stops talking with her close friends), she might feel shame around her behavior. The shame is because she sees her behavior as wrong and misaligned with her identity, standards, and expectations as a friend.

You can probably see how shame ends up being more deeply rooted than guilt. In fact, you can think of guilt as a beginning feeling for shame, and shame as a reflection of internalized guilt. Because shame is internalized to be about who you are, and not just what you did, it can lead to depression, decreased confidence, and lower self-esteem. Of course, it can also negatively influence your identity and make you question your overall understanding of yourself.

Although guilt can be helpful, shame is never helpful. Whether it's correctly attributed to your behavior or not, shame is harmful because it makes you think there's something wrong with who you are. It makes you question what you deserve, which then impacts what you believe you should have, including relationships with other people. You'll hear more about this in chapter 9, as it relates to intimacy, but the way you view yourself and others impacts the way you choose to connect (or not connect) with other people.

Where Guilt and Shame Come From

So why do people feel guilt over things that they should not? Throughout this book, you have learned how some of your thoughts develop from a young age—for example, thoughts around trust and safety. You have also learned how your understanding of experiences, such as trust and safety, are influenced by domestic violence. Thoughts and experiences of guilt and shame develop, and are influenced, in similar ways.

From an early age, you were taught to take responsibility for your actions. When you broke something as a kid, you were told to be honest and say what you did—not to blame it on your sibling, cousin, or friend next door. As you journeyed into adulthood, you likely learned the importance of stepping back, assessing an experience, and understanding your role in it. In fact, you were probably taught to do that in all of your relationships. Doing this is about taking responsibility.

Looking back and assessing your role is a helpful and useful skill to have. It can contribute to positive growth in a variety of relationships, including romantic, friendship, family, collegial, and other relationships. However, if you think that the control you have over yourself is similar to control over other people's behaviors, you might unintentionally blame yourself for others' behaviors—feeling guilt and shame about them.

From an early age you probably also learned that both people, in any type of relationship, have some responsibility for what occurs within their relationship. How many times have you heard the phrase "It takes two"? Most people will say it takes two people to be in communication with each other, and to be in relationship with each other, and that it takes two people to get to the point of ending the relationship.

As you have seen in other chapters, there is a helpful and unhelpful side to these types of messages and lessons. The unhelpful side is taking responsibility for something that is not your fault and blaming yourself when you should blame your abusive partner. As you look back on the relationship, it can be natural to wonder where your ownership of what happened lies. It's also important to remember that abuse that happens *to* you is not something you need to own.

Abusive partners manipulate you into thinking their behavior is your fault, that you should feel guilt and shame over it. When an abusive partner tells you that you brought the abuse on yourself, or that you make them act the way they do, they are manipulating your emotions and making you feel guilty. When an abusive partner tells you no one else will want you or care about you because of what you're doing to cause the abuse, they are manipulating your emotions and making you feel shame. In these examples, they are *victim blaming*. You can see how that influences your feelings of guilt and shame.

An abusive partner isolating you also sets up the conditions for shame to set in. You saw that in Assayiah's (from chapter 1) and Zara's stories. Perhaps you have experienced it as well.

When your friends and family are not present to know what is happening in the relationship, or to fully understand the extent of the abuse, they cannot remind you that the abuse is not your fault. They also cannot remind you of who you are and the strength you hold. Abusive partners intentionally remove you from this type of support, which allows the guilt to develop and the shame to set in.

You might even have felt guilt and shame for coming forward about the abuse. Sometimes survivors feel pressure to protect their abusive partner from other people's perceptions of them. You saw one example of the desire to protect an abusive partner in Yasmine's experience (from chapter 4). That experience was connected to her partner's safety, but feelings of guilt and shame can also be connected to the partner's reputation. Perhaps you worried about coming forward because you thought others would view your partner negatively, or that it would ruin their reputation, standing in the community, or career. But remember: their behavior controls their future. Caretaking may be a natural part of your identity, in ways that you may have begun exploring in this book, but you should not have to protect an abusive partner from the consequences of their own actions.

These feelings can also continue to linger after you have left the abusive relationship. It takes time to unpack why you feel shame, and to learn strategies for changing it. You are reading this book, so you're already headed in the right direction. However, some survivors feel so much shame that they don't talk about the abusive relationship or seek any help, even after leaving. This silence can manifest in deeper feelings of shame when it's given more time to settle in.

Use the next section of this chapter to explore and understand the ways you can let go of guilt and shame, as you continue to heal from domestic violence.

Overcoming Guilt and Shame

There are four things you can practice to help you overcome guilt and shame in your life. You can reevaluate your guilt, remember who you are, let go of expectations, and practice self-forgiveness.

Reevaluate Your Guilt

Because of the harmful nature of guilt (and eventually shame), it's important to evaluate any guilty feelings you have by asking yourself if the behavior you feel guilty about is connected to your actions or someone else's. If you feel guilty about something you did or caused, then you can work through that guilt, as it may belong to you. However, if you feel guilty about something you didn't do and didn't cause (like violence and abuse toward you), you can work toward remembering that fact and reattribute the blame to the correct person (your abusive partner).

In doing this, you must be aware of the fact that the abuse was not your fault. You have read this many times, but it's important to read it again. There is nothing you can do to warrant another person being abusive. Abusers are responsible for their own behaviors. Don't misattribute their behavior to your own. Don't take responsibility for their actions.

Journal Prompts

Take a moment to write down the things you feel guilty about. Then, mark which of those things were based on your actions or your abusive partner's actions. Decide if you want to hold on to, or let go of, the guilt that was not based on your actions.

Now highlight, or otherwise indicate, the things you feel guilty about that *are* connected to your actions and *were* in your control. Now, consider if you want to change those things. If you want to change them, guilt can be helpful and motivating for that change. If you don't want to change them, you can reevaluate if you want to also let go of that guilt.

Remember Who You Are

Because shame is so deeply connected to how you understand yourself, your worth, and your value, it's important to remember who you are outside of the situations you feel shame about. You are not your situation. Try not to internalize that a *situation* is now your actual character.

Journal Prompts

Consider these questions and reflect on them in your journal.

1. How might *what you do* be different than *who you are?*

2. How might an action be different from your character?

3. How might a situation reflect a moment and not your lifetime?

Keep in mind, being in an unhealthy relationship does not make you a broken person. It doesn't mean you're incapable of being in different types of relationships, or that there is something wrong with you that will cause future abusive relationships to occur. Remember, your worth is not tied to someone else's treatment of you. Remember back to how you saw yourself before the trauma of the abusive relationship. Take a moment to list some of your qualities. Then, reflect on what aspects of those qualities are still with you today.

Consider this: you're not the worst of what you felt. There is a difference between how you feel and who you are. For example, you may feel embarrassed about having been/being in an abusive relationship, but it doesn't mean you're an embarrassment as a person. You may feel bad about losing connection with people you care about, but it doesn't mean you're a bad person. Feelings are not equivalent to who you are.

Let Go of Expectations

As we have discussed, guilt and shame are connected to perceptions of right and wrong, which are guided by your moral, social, cultural, and religious expectations. Take a moment to consider which of these expectations are helpful for your healing, and which are harmful. Also, consider which of these expectations are truly yours and which are others' expectations that you're holding on to. This task is important because you may feel shame related to expectations that are not yours, or that you don't desire to have. This may ease the process of letting go of those expectations.

Journal Prompts

What are your expectations about what relationships should look like? Do you expect relationships to continue no matter what happens in them? Do you expect yourself or your partner to control finances, schedules, social events, family and friend interactions, etc.? Does it matter if you're dating or married? Where do those expectations come from? Are they helpful, harmful, yours, or others'? Are they contributing to your shame? Do you want to keep them or let them go? Consider these questions and note your answers in your journal.

Practice Self-Forgiveness

Forgive yourself for all the should've, could've, would've statements that torment you. Forgive yourself for all the things you believe you should have done differently, or could have prevented, or would have changed. The past cannot be undone, but you can learn from it and change what you can moving forward.

For example, you cannot change that your children may have witnessed abuse, or that you disconnected from others because of the emotional state you were in from being abused. However, you can change the current connection you have to your children, other family, or friends. You have the power to improve it.

Consider this: you did the best that you could, given the situation that you were in. No one tries to do their worst or be their worst. This applies to you, too. Experiencing domestic violence can take an emotional, mental, physical, and spiritual toll on you. As you reflect on your own life during that time, try to think about your behavior and actions as being the best that you could do, given where you were at the time. Doing this will allow you to lessen the guilt that you feel, which is important if the guilt is going to be motivating and not debilitating. If you continue to stay in a place of overwhelming guilt, it will be too debilitating to move out of, and it will continue to grow into shame. Instead, forgive yourself for what was done so you can move forward.

Also, allow yourself to change as you need to. Self-forgiveness requires you to accept your experiences as they have happened, and also allow yourself to be more than those experiences. This is connected to the practice of remembering who you are. Remember: trauma can change many things about a person. Allow yourself the freedom to explore the new aspects of yourself. See if you can let go of old expectations and establish new ones that feel more congruent with who you are and where you are.

Lastly, talk about your process of self-forgiveness and healing with your trusted loved ones. Silence can often foster more shame, in the same way isolation can deepen shame. You did the best you could, and you don't have to hide in silence or in shame about it. Allow your support system in. They can remind you why you deserve self-forgiveness.

Reflective Moment

Take a moment to check in and see how you're feeling, now that you've finished reading and reflecting on the meaning of guilt and shame. You've thought about how they develop, and how they may be helpful or unhelpful for you. You also learned four practical strategies for helping you overcome guilt and shame. Use these strategies as encouragement and support on your journey toward healing.

Additionally, you read examples—such as in Zara's experience— that may have triggered some of your own memories. Remember that the emotions that arise with your memories are okay. At any time, you can practice the grounding exercise that you learned earlier on in the book. You can also take a break, pace yourself, and of course, come back.

The next chapter is about recognizing your power and reclaiming control in your life. Before you turn to that chapter, take a moment to check in and reflect on what feelings and thoughts have come up for you in this chapter. Use the journal prompts to guide you through.

Journal Prompts

1. What do you feel guilty about that you also have control over? How would you like to address that guilt or change the actions related to it?

2. How have misplaced guilt and shame influenced you? Have they impacted your relationships, career, self-esteem, or other areas? Reflect on the areas of your life where you see the presence or consequence of misplaced guilt and shame.

3. What strategy for addressing guilt and shame seems most important to you? Which ones can you commit to working on starting now?

CHAPTER 8

Recognizing Your Power and Reclaiming Control

The most common way people give up their power is by thinking they don't have any.

—Alice Walker

Themes of power and control, as we've discussed, are central to understanding the ways you have been impacted by domestic violence. As you read this chapter, remember that your power is present within you, and that there is no greater example of this than your ability to take control over your life, leave the abusive relationship, and choose a path toward healing. No matter where you are in the process of leaving, or on the path toward healing, you likely have more power than you think.

Self-Power and Other-Power

Two types of power are relevant to a domestic-abuse context: self-power (also known as "power to") and other-power (also known as "power over"). *Self-power* refers to your belief that you can solve problems, resist oppression, pursue self-determined interests, and meet new challenges. When you have a high level of self-power, you can act according to your free will and effectively manage your own thoughts, feelings, and behavior. The level of power you have is commonly influenced by your age, education level, employment status, and the economic resources you have access to.

Domestic violence can render you virtually powerless. After experiencing abuse in your relationship, you might notice a desire to reestablish control over your life. Sometimes this desire can go to the extreme, such that you believe you must control everything, or such that if any area of your life feels out of control, you assume you have lost all control. There is a tendency to try and control everything in your life, including your emotions.

On the other hand, you may experience the opposite extreme: believing you're completely powerless. When you feel you have no control, you might become passive in your approach to life—choosing not to pursue the degree, go after the promotion you want, or start something new, because you fear you'll fail. Feeling powerless can create hesitancy to make any decisions, because you assume you don't deserve the desired outcome, or you believe it won't happen anyway.

But no matter how powerless or out of control you may feel, in reality (outside of an abusive or manipulative situation), you *always* have some measure of power and control in your life. It's simply a matter of exploring and expanding your control to a point where you feel empowered to influence your experiences and the direction of your life.

Other-power refers to your belief that you can (or cannot) influence, control, change, or manipulate another person's behavior. In the aftermath of domestic violence, it's not uncommon for survivors to feel compelled to have complete control in new and preexisting relationships. This might result in difficulty working effectively in teams or partnerships, sharing decision-making with others, or a quickness to cut a relationship off if you feel uncertain about its future.

After having power completely stripped from you in an abusive relationship, it can feel scary to relinquish any power in the future. However, sharing power and control is essential to having healthy and balanced relationships.

Power and Control from a Young Age

Power, from a young person's perspective, can be thought of in two ways. One way to look at the themes of power and control is to consider the ways you express them in your everyday life. This expression will have grown and changed over time. Another way to look at power and control is through the thoughts that developed from a young age and changed or solidified over time.

The act of displaying control within your own life is something you have done since you were a child. From a young age, you began to express your ability to direct your own path, do things your own way, and express how you wanted others to do things as well. The toddler "terrible twos" are an important time of learning to exercise power and control. This is the age when children really begin to express themselves and their preferences for how they want things done. This process actually develops before the age of two, but occurs more often and with more assertiveness around two. These memories may be far back in your mind and not something you consider on a regular basis, but they are likely when you first began to learn about the power and control that you have over yourself and your environment.

Try to recall what you were like as a young child, maybe around age four or five. How did people describe you? What was important for you to do or have? Even if the words "power" and "control" were not used, how would your family have described your preferences and choices around the way you wanted things? Perhaps you insisted on walking when people tried to carry you. Maybe you were clear about the foods that you would and would not eat, or the people you would or would not be around. Maybe you needed to pick out your own clothes or begin to choose your own activities. At some point, you might have said the phrase "I don't want to, and you can't make me." These are early methods of exercising control, and at each stage of life, you began to learn new methods to exercise control.

As you grew older, your decision-making power likely grew stronger. You were able to make decisions without asking permission or needing assistance. In fact, from the time you first learned to make a decision until the present moment, you have made countless decisions and choices that you have control over. For example, you likely decided what you were going to wear today, and what you would eat. You may be in a career you have chosen for yourself, or even looking to change jobs based on your desired employment. You chose to read this book, and to set aside time to focus on your healing. You may not even think about these daily exercises of power and control in your decision-making process, but they are present.

You've learned about the ways trauma and abuse confirm or disrupt the lessons you learned as a child (e.g., your sense of safety and trust). They can do the same to your sense of power and control. Perhaps you have never seen yourself as a powerful person. You might have grown up in a household where you felt little to no power or control. Abusive relationships in adulthood might further confirm these messages from childhood.

Or perhaps instead you have always seen yourself as a powerful person, but having an abusive partner actively work to make you feel powerless disrupted things. You may have experienced yourself as able to control your life and make your own decisions, until an abusive partner took away the things that allowed you to express control. For example, they may have forbade you to work, sabotaged your employment, or otherwise prevented you from being able to make money, to be independent from them.

Abusive partners intentionally exert their own power and control over you in order to make you feel less powerful and less in control of your life. It's important to remind yourself that your power continues to exist within you, despite someone trying to take it away.

Being free from an abusive relationship will require that you relearn the sense of power you once had, if you did once feel you had it. Being free will also require you to relearn feeling out of control, if that was your childhood experience. In very similar ways to how you did in earlier stages of your life, you will again learn to exercise and negotiate your power and control over yourself and your environment in new ways. You have grown in your understanding of relationships and interactions, since childhood, and your new understandings will influence how freely you approach this task of relearning.

Black Women's Control Dilemmas

Power and control dynamics in domestic violence are complicated by the larger social context of systemic inequality, in which Black people have less power and control. Compared to White people, Black people hold fewer political leadership positions, are underrepresented in professional roles, have less wealth, and are paid less than Whites at every education level. All of this equates to less power to change unfair policies and structures, less control to end discrimination, and less access to resources. It's important to consider the impact of this larger sociocultural context of inequality, in considering what makes domestic violence power and control dynamics unique for you as a Black woman.

Psychologist Dr. Jennifer Gomez developed *cultural betrayal trauma theory* to explain how societal trauma, like discrimination, creates the context for interpersonal trauma within marginalized groups. Because Black people, as a community, are all impacted by societal trauma, we develop a shared sense of connection and solidarity that bonds us together, to help us resist the pain and harm often associated with being

Black in America. Thus, *cultural betrayal* occurs when a Black person victimizes or violates the trust of another Black person. This violation is more painful than it would have been had the abuser been from the majority or other culture, because of the intracultural trust implicit within the Black community.

If the perpetrator was a member of the Black community, domestic violence is a form of cultural betrayal that can negatively impact the way you see yourself in relationship to the Black community, or the way you view other members of the Black community who share similar characteristics to the person who violated you. A desire to not "betray" the Black community can cause you, as a survivor, to feel torn between a rock and a hard place, when it comes to talking about your past experiences or involving the criminal justice system.

Involving the criminal justice system is one way that people might tell you to take your power back. It's a valid method of exerting control where you can and showing that your abusive partner didn't take all of your power. However, as we've discussed, it can also be very challenging to do if your partner was also Black. Yasmine, back in chapter 4, was fearful of calling the police even when she needed help. She was concerned about what it would mean for the safety of her, her partner (even though he was abusive), and their child. We can imagine she might have also felt uncertainty about involving her partner in the criminal justice system, in general.

Have you experienced this apprehension to involve your partner in the criminal justice system? Without judging yourself or applying other people's standards, take a moment to think about where your apprehension might have come from. How would you *like* to feel about it? Where would you like to stand, related to your power and control in this area?

Black Women's Struggle for Power

Back in chapter 1, we discussed the societal issues that have contributed to the dynamics of domestic violence, including gender-role stereotypes as contributing factors to people's perceptions of how relationships should operate. You read about the societal expectations that women be passive, polite, and avoid conflict, while men, on the other hand, voice strong opinions, take the lead, and ultimately show their power and ability to control situations (including relationships).

As a Black woman, you may feel an additional pressure to control your emotions so you're not portrayed as the "angry Black woman." You may have been asked to monitor your own feelings of hurt, sadness, anger, and pain because they are too much for others to handle—being asked to control something that others are really trying to control for you, in their requests for a muted version of yourself. For many spiritual or religious Black women, this idea may be heightened by the notions of who should lead and who should follow in a household. Some Black women are expected to be the matriarch in their family and to run the household, but to do so behind the scenes so they appear to have less power than they really do.

These messages are about the hidden strength of the Black woman—about the pressure to have power, and to exercise control, but to do so in a way that is hidden and non-threatening. Give yourself permission to let these messages go as you regain the power and control that relationships and societal messages have tried to steal from you.

Following are some practical ways to enhance a sense of power and control.

Allow for Vulnerability

Continue to think about letting some of these messages go, as you work to regain a sense of power and control. What would it be like to let go of messages that teach you to be strong in your resilience but silent in your pain? What would it mean to let go of messages that ask you to lead, but only in ways that make it appear as if you're actually following? How would it feel to hold onto the message that you have power but don't have to be all-powerful?

Letting go of these messages and replacing them with a more balanced view of your power is important to the healing process. For example, the message that you're strong. You have shown that. You are also allowed to feel pain and to express that pain, even if it makes others feel uncomfortable. Your tears are valid. You don't have to completely control these emotions by silencing them, so as not to appear to be an angry Black woman. Maybe you're angry—and that anger is warranted.

Letting go of the old messages means allowing yourself to be free in your own experience. It means not being controlled by other people's ideas of who you should be, how you should act, or what your relationships should look like. It means determining those things for yourself. That also requires vulnerability.

To regain a sense of power and control, recognize that you don't have to be all-powerful. In fact, you cannot be all-powerful, completely in control, *and* have the balanced view of power that is needed for healing. There is power in displaying true emotions, and of course there is also power in vulnerability.

It can be hard to be vulnerable as a Black woman, because you may feel that you're giving away power that you have worked hard to earn. It can be difficult to acknowledge being victimized, because it may seem incongruent with your sense of being strong and in control. Recognizing your pain may feel at odds with your sense of being able to "hold it together." However, allowing for the vulnerability of these experiences, and all the emotions that come with them, is needed to regain power and control. The vulnerability allows you to let go of the messages and narratives that people and society have placed on you and to live your life in ways that are more authentic to yourself. It's much easier to feel power over your life when that life is true to who you are.

Identify Your Control

Because things were so entirely outside your control in the domestic violence relationship, it can seem like you're still in that space, where nothing is within your control. While it's true that many things in life *are* beyond your control, there are some things that you do have control over. Regaining a sense of power and control in your life requires a shift in focus. When you constantly focus on the things that are outside your control, you're more likely to feel stuck, disappointed, anxious, and disempowered. When you shift your focus to the things that are in your control, you will feel less confined and more empowered.

Journal Prompts

To help you become aware of the things within your control, grab your journal and make a list of all the situations that challenge you or cause strain and tension in your life, known as *stressors*. Stressors can make you feel powerless and out of control, because they often cause physiological changes inside your body. When you're faced with stressors, your body's stress response is triggered, and your body reacts with a wide range of symptoms ranging from sweating to extreme panic. You might even notice some mild changes happening in your body as you write down your list of stressors, which is normal.

Now, take the list of stressors you identified and split the larger list into two smaller lists titled "Stressors Within My Control" and "Stressors Outside of My Control." Begin with the list outside of your control first. For this list, you will want to write down all the things that typically (but not always) *happen to you* that are outside your control. Some examples might be: other people's actions, thoughts, and feelings; the weather; getting sick; loss of a job; not being selected for an opportunity you applied for; trauma memories that pop into your head throughout the day; emotions you experience; thoughts you have; aging; painful loss of a loved one.

Next, move to the "Stressors Within My Control" list. Typically (but not always) *your responses* to the things on the other list *are* within your control. Here, include all the ways you handle and think about the stressors on the list. This includes your response to your thoughts and feelings; the effort you put into pursuing your goals; the mindset or attitude you bring to situations; what you say and do that influences others; how much time you spend focusing on stressors outside of your control; any tendencies toward procrastination; and the actions you take to care for your mind, body, and spirit.

With a complete list of stressors within and outside of your control, think about how you can start to feel more in control. You've probably heard some version of the Serenity Prayer: *"God, grant me the serenity to accept the things I cannot change, the courage to change the things I can, and the wisdom to know the difference."* This simple statement highlights the key to how to handle things that are outside of your control: accept them. Acceptance doesn't mean the things outside of your control are wanted, fun, fair, deserved, or comfortable. It just means acknowledging that these things happen. Once you learn to accept that things outside of your control will happen, you can focus your valuable energy and attention on the things you can control.

Now let's go back to the "Stressors Within My Control" list. First, take a moment to take in your list. It can be freeing and exciting to realize how much power and control you actually have in your day-to-day life, after going so long feeling like you have none. Next to each item, write down the response that would help you to feel powerful and in control when that stressor comes. For example, say a stressor you wrote down is: *How I respond to my annoying coworker.* Maybe this coworker is too negative, uncooperative, or gossips all the time. Some ways you could respond to restore a sense of power or control in the situation include: making a direct request that your coworker change the behavior (or not engage in it in your presence); shifting your attention away from the behavior by wearing earbuds and listening to calming music; removing yourself from the situation (if you can); or choosing to ignore the behavior.

The key to remember is this: you get to decide how you want to respond. In and of itself, this is empowering. It may take you some trial and error to determine the response that leads to the best outcome for you and your mental health, but you stay in the driver's seat if you remember that the choice is yours.

Learn to Share Power

William Booth, preacher and founder of the Salvation Army, is credited with saying, *"The greatness of a man's power is the measure of his surrender."* This quote makes clear that power is more about how much you're willing to give up than how tightly you cling to control. In relationships, you might think of this as a willingness to be vulnerable and not always have things go your way with a partner, family member, or friend. When you share power, you're willing to follow someone else's leadership, learn from others, take other people's needs or ideas into consideration when making choices, and work collaboratively to make decisions in the best interest of all people involved. Similarly, in relationships with shared power, both partners feel comfortable initiating and leading discussions about issues or decisions that need to be made.

When you've survived an experience as disempowering as domestic violence, one of your priorities may be to never experience a sense of disempowerment again. You might find it challenging to share power in relationships, for fear that "if you give them an inch, they'll take a mile." But relationships where there is any imbalance of power are unhealthy and not likely to last. Being willing to share power in your relationships is key to your health and happiness. But how do you do this?

Remember, power is the ability to influence another person's thoughts, feelings, and behavior so they align with your preferences. It's also about your ability to resist being influenced by another person. In healthy relationships, both parties feel heard, seen, respected, and valued. Both people feel comfortable bringing up issues in the relationship and contributing ideas to problem-solving discussions, and both individuals are willing to lead and follow each other.

The Search Institute, a research center dedicated to youth and family development, has identified four practical ways to share power in relationships: show respect; include people in decisions that affect them; collaborate to solve problems and reach goals; and provide opportunities for both relational partners to lead. Although these tips were designed with families in mind, they can be beneficial for all relationship types.

Show Respect: When you respect someone, you have a deep admiration for them and highly regard their thoughts, knowledge, qualities, and accomplishments. Respect is communicated through actions such as honoring boundaries, listening to their ideas or concerns (even when you disagree), and not violating their rights. One example of how you can work on sharing power in your relationship is engaging in a conversation about a topic where you and the person you're in a relationship with (whether it be a child, family member, partner, or friend) share a differing perspective on an issue and demonstrate verbal and nonverbal respect for each other.

Include People in Decisions That Affect Them: Inclusion occurs in relationships when both individuals have equal access to laying out options for problem-solving and guiding decision-making about a variety of issues like planning new activities, what to eat, how to spend downtime, how to spend money, or where to send children to school. If you want to challenge yourself with sharing power in the domain of inclusion, identify an area of decision-making where you typically make decisions and, instead of making the decision alone, ask for input from the people who will be impacted by it.

Collaborate to Solve Problems and Reach Goals: Collaboration is all about working together to reach a common goal or create something new. You can try out collaboration in your relationships by examining the pros and cons of a decision, with the help of a relationship partner.

Provide Opportunities for Both Relational Partners to Lead: Leadership is the ability to take initiative and move people toward a vision, mission, or goal. When you create opportunities for relationship partners to lead, it strengthens the bond, boosts their confidence, and relieves you of the responsibility of having to always take initiative for things to get done.

Define Power for Yourself

The way you define something will inevitably impact how you relate to it. If you feel skeptical about this, consider the behavior of someone who loves mayonnaise, versus someone who is severely allergic to mayonnaise. The person who loves mayonnaise probably defines it with words like "delicious" and "tasty" and, as a result, they likely go the extra mile to find ways to include it in their meals. The person who is allergic might describe mayonnaise as "disgusting" and "pungent" and as a result be vigilant in avoiding ingesting it. The way each person defined it determined how they engaged with it. The same can be said for power—how you think about it will determine your desires, feelings, and behaviors related to it. It can also determine if you see yourself as having power or not.

If you took a poll of a hundred people in your community, you might get a hundred different definitions of what it means to have power. In a domestic violence relationship, you likely had little say or ability to define things for yourself. Your goal may have been to conform to the way your abusive partner defined things, to keep yourself safe and alive. But now that you're no longer in the relationship, you have the freedom to define things on your own terms—and power is no exception.

Journal Prompts

Take a moment to explore the following questions:

1. What does power mean to me?

2. When was the last time I felt powerful? How did I know I was feeling power (e.g., bodily sensations, emotions, behaviors)?

3. What actions can I take to help myself feel empowered in the future?

4. What do I need from my environment and support system to help me feel empowered?

Once you have developed your own definition of power and what it means to be powerful, you can begin to expand your view of yourself as it relates to power. Consider in what ways you possess power. In other words, what kinds of influence do you have and what abilities do you have to resist other people's influence? When answering this question, think about the following domains: womanhood, parenting, social and family relationships, romantic relationships, career, spirituality and religion, physical health, and mental health.

Reflective Moment: Recognize Your Resilience and Survival

As you have read, it's important to recognize the power and control you have had, and continue to have to this day. You couldn't control what someone else did to you, but you did have enough control over your life to begin the process of leaving, and you have! You have power over yourself and can control your own responses and reactions. You can control how you choose to move forward from here.

Your ability to use your power and control is tied to your resilience. You showed resilience every day you survived in an abusive relationship, and you have continued to survive after it. That type of resilience is a process of coping and coming back to yourself, despite external or internal messages that have made you feel less powerful. We hope that you are working on letting go of those messages.

Journal Prompts

1. How has your understanding of your power changed after reading this chapter?

2. As you reflect back on your ability to leave the abusive relationship, what was important for you to have control over? How important is that now?

3. What aspects of your power and control are important to attend to in current, or future, relationships? Those relationships can be intimate, but they can also be with peers, family, or colleagues.

CHAPTER 9

Choosing Intimacy

One of the best guides to how to be self-loving is to give ourselves the love we are often dreaming about receiving from others.

—bell hooks

When you hear the word "intimacy," what is the first thought that comes to mind? For many, intimacy is synonymous with sex, but it's actually much broader. Key features of intimacy include emotional closeness, honesty, support, respect, open communication, vulnerability, safety, and both physical and non-physical affection. For survivors of domestic violence, two types of intimacy are impacted: intimacy with self and intimacy with others.

Self-intimacy involves your ability to cope, soothe, and care for yourself. *Other-intimacy* involves your ability to feel close, vulnerable, and connected to another person. Other-intimacy includes nonsexual intimacy with family and friends, as well as sexual intimacy. Feelings of intimacy with others can originate from honest self-disclosure, emotional expressiveness, freely sharing differences of opinion in a respectful way, physical contact, sexual contact, sharing activities, receiving unconditional support and acceptance, feeling understood and appreciated, and warmth.

Intimate relationships differ from other types of relationships in six ways: knowledge, caring, interdependence, mutuality, trust, and commitment. Intimate partners:

- Know more confidential and personal information about each other than people who are not in intimate relationships.

- Care for one another and demonstrate that care through physical (e.g., hugging, kissing, holding hands) and nonphysical affection (e.g., saying "I love you," smiling, looking into each other's eyes, providing emotional or other types of support).

- Impact each other in meaningful ways. They need each other and their actions influence each other.

- Tend to view themselves as a part of a team, with shared, overlapping identities.

- Trust each other. They expect the other to be responsive, treat them kindly, and act with their best interests in mind.

- Display commitment to the relationship by investing time, effort, and resources into the stability of the relationship.

It's important to note that these qualities of intimate relationships can exist in your intimate relationship with yourself. Also, all six qualities are not required for a relationship to be considered an intimate one. However, intimate relationships tend to be most satisfying when all six qualities are present.

For some Black women, self- and other-intimacy are disrupted by domestic violence. After leaving an abusive partner, it's not uncommon for women to feel emotionally disconnected from themselves, lose interest in sex and close relationships, lose trust in themselves and others, develop a negative image of their bodies, and experience intrusive thoughts when feeling vulnerable or during sexual intimacy.

For others, self- and other-intimacy never fully developed. Early sexual experiences can shape adult practices around intimacy with self and others. If you grew up in a household where you were told explicitly or implicitly that touching your body is sinful, sex is problematic, sexual play and curiosity are wrong, or "sexual feelings should be ignored rather than understood and enjoyed" (Wyatt 1997), you may have difficulty allowing yourself to be intimate with yourself or another person. If you were sexually violated in childhood or didn't have the opportunity to observe healthy, affectionate relationships growing up, that could negatively impact intimacy.

In her pivotal book *Stolen Women: Reclaiming Our Sexuality, Taking Back Our Lives*, Dr. Gail Wyatt tells the story of Erin, a thirty-four-year-old Black woman whose mother would tell her she "needed a man" whenever she was in a bad mood growing up. If you grew up hearing this type of narrative, it could lead you to believe that self-intimacy is wrong or impossible. This type of messaging also suggests that you should rely on others to meet your emotional or intimacy needs. This can create tension for you if you resist the notion that you "need a man" to be happy, yet still have the desire for a truly intimate, mutually respectful and fulfilling relationship. Restrictive views of sexuality and societal stereotypes that portray Black girls and women as sexually loose or promiscuous could also create confusion or hesitancy around intimacy. You might not be as free with your sexuality as you would like to be, due to concerns about validating certain stereotypes.

Although reduced intimacy is common among survivors of domestic violence, some survivors of domestic violence become overly intimate, which can manifest in unsafe sexual practices, multiple sexual partners, or compulsive sexual activity. In most instances, hypersexuality is engaged in with the intent of coping with painful emotions, feeling comfort, distracting oneself from painful thoughts or emotions, punishing oneself, resolving low self-esteem, gaining power and control, or as a substitution for emotional intimacy.

For Black women, intimacy after domestic violence can also be complicated by cultural values and expectations about gender roles. In the Black community, women are often expected to put others' needs before their own. If this was your experience, you might find that you became adept at putting your intimacy needs on the back burner, so much so that you view intimacy as something done solely to attract or please others. It may be difficult to wrap your head around the concept of self-intimacy. In extreme cases, you might even lose the ability to identify your intimacy wants and needs. It's not uncommon for Black women's decisions around intimacy to be shaped primarily by outside forces, including friends, parents, religious institutions, and societal pressures.

One aspect of intimacy with others is the ability to be vulnerable. Vulnerability includes being honest about what you need and how you feel. This can be challenging for survivors of domestic violence when vulnerability has previously been unsafe. A history of sexual or physical abuse or sexual harassment can lead to expectations of being harshly punished for being honest about your needs and wants in a relationship. You might feel hesitant to speak up for yourself, for fear that you will be harmed. In sexual relationships, you might be unwilling to have discussions with your partner about preferred sexual practices or the use of contraceptives—which could result in sexual activities that could expose you to an STI or lead to an unwanted pregnancy, or feelings of shame or guilt.

Domestic violence can also block self- and other-intimacy by influencing the type of treatment you grew accustomed to. If you're used to being put down, criticized, or emotionally neglected by a domestically violent partner, you may be more prone to withholding care and compassion from yourself, or choosing partners who are not available for healthy intimacy. If you were forced to be sexually intimate with a partner against your will, you may have learned to disconnect emotionally during sex. A history of manipulation can block intimacy by causing you to be overly suspicious of new non-abusive partners, too.

Reclaim Intimacy With Yourself and Others

Despite the challenges you face as a Black woman who has survived domestic violence, you *can* reclaim intimacy with yourself and others. The first step to reclaiming intimacy is educating yourself. For a variety of reasons, you may have received misinformation about healthy intimacy with yourself and others. Believing myths and misconceptions about intimacy can shape your desires, practices, and expectations, and can negatively influence decision-making. Obtaining specific information about healthy relationships, typical sexual development, and normal body functioning can help you take the first steps toward reclaiming intimacy with yourself and others.

Accurate information may be obtained from medical and mental health professionals, books, and reputable online resources. Some sources you might begin with: *Longing to Tell: Black Women Talk About Sexuality and Intimacy* by Tricia Rose, *Stolen Women: Reclaiming Our Sexuality, Taking Back Our Lives* by Dr. Gail Wyatt, and the California Wellness Foundation Sexual Health Toolkit for Black Women: *RoyalTea: Hot Tips to Sip for Sexual Empowerment.*

Self-knowledge is also key to developing increased intimacy with yourself. It's important to understand how your experience of domestic violence impacted your feelings of intimacy with yourself and others. Journaling can be a powerful strategy for increasing your awareness of how intimacy was impacted by domestic violence.

Journal Prompts

Grab a journal and consider the prompts that follow. First, though, we want to acknowledge that the prompts will likely bring up a variety of feelings and realizations. Go at your own pace, take breaks as needed, and revisit the grounding and breathing exercises shared in previous chapters.

1. Do you believe you're capable of coping with negative life events?

2. When you're emotionally triggered, how do you comfort yourself?

3. On a scale from 0–10, where 0 = not at all comfortable and 10 = extremely comfortable, how comfortable do you feel soothing yourself when you're experiencing physical or emotional pain? How comfortable are you being soothed by others?

4. What do you say to yourself when you feel sick, overwhelmed, or exhausted?

5. How good are you at labeling your emotions and communicating them to others?

6. Do you avoid going deep in relationships? What are your typical avoidance strategies?

7. Do you often feel anxious or suspicious in social situations? If so, what are you anticipating will happen?

8. Do you often isolate yourself from other people?

9. How do you feel about letting people get to know the real "you"?

10. How do you feel about being vulnerable during conversations with others? During sex? Examples of vulnerability include making eye contact, telling someone you love them before you know the feeling is mutual, sharing something you're embarrassed about, crying in front of others, or

telling someone when they have done or said something to hurt you or let you down.

11. Do you say what you really want, think, and feel in relationships? If not, what gets in the way?

12. How do you feel about asking for comfort and support from others?

13. Do you worry about being rejected, abandoned, or abused in your current relationships? What do you do to protect your- .self from feeling rejected, abandoned, or abused?

14. Do you have a fear of being alone?

15. Are you able to enjoy your own company without feeling empty or lonely?

16. Are you needy or demanding in relationships with partners, family, and friends?

17. Do you believe you can have satisfying intimate relationships?

18. Do you enter new relationships feeling suspicious that you will be betrayed, abused, or taken advantage of?

19. How do you show others (e.g., children, partners, family, friends) that you care about them?

Answering these questions will allow you to begin noticing patterns of unhealthy intimacy that may benefit from being addressed with a mental health professional. For example, if you notice that you're overly reliant on external sources of comfort (e.g., constantly seeking reassurance from others, food, alcohol, spending large amounts of money) to calm you down when you feel overwhelmed or triggered, it might be a sign that you would benefit from developing self-intimacy skills. Similarly, if you notice that you always feel lonely, empty, or disconnected from others, have difficulty letting people get close to you, or avoid telling people what you need, you might benefit from developing other-intimacy skills. Relationships thrive when you're willing to communicate openly and vulnerably, ask for what you need, and let people in.

Unlearn Abusive Messages

Another step to reclaiming intimacy is unlearning messages and beliefs that resulted from abuse and trauma. It's not uncommon for Black women to leave an abusive relationship feeling as though they are unlovable or incapable of having a safe and satisfying romantic relationship in the future. Some people walk away from domestic violence believing that all men have negative intentions or motives; others may vow to never again allow themselves to be vulnerable or need anyone. These types of beliefs can get in the way of intimacy by influencing the way you approach future relationships.

Journal Prompts

It can be helpful to write down what messages you learned about relationships from your experience with domestic violence. Grab your journal and answer this question: How did experiencing domestic violence change your perceptions of yourself and other people?

Be Willing to Share Your Thoughts and Feelings

There can be experiences in a new non-abusive relationship that remind you of an abusive ex. Some partners may have a physical appearance, personality traits, or mannerisms that remind you of your abuser. Others may have ways of touching you during sex or intimate moments that trigger automatic thoughts about a past abusive partner. When thoughts of abuse are triggered, it can be easy to mistakenly believe that your new partner is just like your abusive ex, or that the new partner intends to harm or abuse you. Your new partner can become the target for anger and resentment that you feel toward your ex. Over time, this can cause your partner to feel hurt, upset, or insulted, and it can slowly erode intimacy.

You can prevent this erosion by sharing thoughts that you're having with your partner. For example, if a new non-abusive partner initiates sex in a way that reminds you of the way your abuser used to force sex on you when you didn't want it, rather than assuming your new partner views you as a sex object or that they don't respect your sexual boundaries, it can be useful to share these thoughts with your partner. Talking to your partner will help you to understand their true motives and intentions, while also helping you to see your partner as they are, rather than relating to them as if they were your abusive ex. Sharing what you're thinking, as opposed to acting on your thoughts, may also prevent you from treating your partner harshly, and may help you feel understood, as well as increasing the sense of intimacy and connection you feel with your partner. You can practice this strategy of talking about your thoughts and assumptions in intimate relationships with family members and friends.

Replace Beliefs That Hold Intimacy Back

Another way to reclaim intimacy in relationships is by examining the helpfulness of beliefs you have developed after experiencing domestic violence. Refer back to your responses to the question *How did experiencing domestic violence change your perceptions of yourself and other people?* For each response, ask yourself: How aligned is this thought with my goals for intimacy? You may find some beliefs are out of alignment with your intimacy goals. For example, if your intimacy goal is to be more affectionate in your relationship with your children, but you're holding on to the thought "Showing affection is a sign of weakness," that may prevent you from getting to a deeper level of intimacy with your children.

When you discover that a thought is not in alignment with your intimacy goals, you might consider replacing that thought with a more helpful one. For example, if your misaligned thought is "I'm unworthy of love and happiness," you might consider replacing that thought with "I have a deep desire to feel loved and be happy." Replacing misaligned thoughts with more-aligned ones can help to restore hope and lead you to take intentional action toward your intimacy goals.

It can also be helpful to reexamine things you learned in childhood about intimacy, which may no longer serve you. For example, if you grew up in a household where you were prohibited from any form of exploratory self-touching, you might feel awkward engaging in masturbation or examining your breasts for lumps. It's important to examine whether holding on to these prohibitions around self-touching is useful today, or potentially creates barriers to pleasure and overall wellness.

Explore Intimacy in New Ways

You may want to reclaim intimacy by giving yourself permission to explore intimacy with yourself and others. This could take a variety of forms. For some, this might look like growing your comfort level with your own company, or experimenting with new ways of soothing yourself that don't involve alcohol or food.

One healthy method of soothing or caring for yourself is self-touch. Touch activates the system in your body responsible for calming you down and helping you to feel safe. Finding the right form of touch for you may take some experimentation. Drawing from a mindful self-compassion program exercise called Supportive Touch, we have listed below a few types of touch you might find calming and supportive.

If you can, set aside fifteen minutes to go through each type of touch, taking note of how it makes you feel. Think of this as "trying on" each type of touch to see how comforting it is, like trying on several pairs of jeans in a fitting room to see which pair fits best. Try to stay with each type of touch for one to two minutes. Really pay attention to how you feel emotionally, and in your body, and to the thoughts or memories that come up with each form of touch. Feel the pressure and warmth of your hand with each touch. Remember to breathe throughout the practice.

1. Hand over your heart

2. One hand on your cheek

3. Both hands on both cheeks

4. Gently rub your arm

5. Give yourself a hug by crossing your arms in front of your body and gently squeezing your upper arms

6. Sitting down, rock yourself slowly and gently from side to side (or back and forth) as if you were gently rocking a baby in your arms

7. Gently rub your chest

8. Place one hand on your belly

9. Place one hand on your belly and the other hand over your heart

10. Cup one hand in the other in your lap

Once you have tried each, note in your journal which forms of touch helped you to feel comforted and safe.

Reach Out for Support

Giving yourself permission to explore intimacy with others could look like reaching out for support when you're feeling sad or upset, asking for help, initiating some form of consensual physical contact that communicates your affection (e.g., hug, hand-holding, gentle head rub), expressing appreciation for what you love and value about another, or having a vulnerable conversation.

Journal Prompts

It's important to explore forms of intimacy that are meaningful to you in the context of relationships that are safe, trusting, and respectful. To get you started thinking about what forms of intimacy you would like to explore, think about your current intimate relationships. Consider how you would like to take your feelings of closeness and connectivity to the next level. Write a list of intimate activities you would like to engage in (e.g., tell someone you love them, kiss a romantic partner, hold hands, engage in mutual pleasurable touching or sex). Next, organize this list of intimate activities into a hierarchy, where the bottom includes activities that you're most comfortable doing and the top includes activities that you would like to be more comfortable doing. Rank each item 0–100, where 0 = extremely comfortable/easy to do and 100 = extremely uncomfortable/difficult to do.

Experimenting with the intimate activities you're less comfortable with can help you feel more comfortable and build confidence. One method for experimenting is called *exposure*. Exposure involves gradually and repeatedly doing safe activities that make you uncomfortable or anxious until you become more comfortable. Beginning at the bottom of your list with the intimacy activity that is comfortable, challenge yourself to engage in that activity as frequently as you can until you're ready to move on to the next activity. As you progress to activities you're less comfortable with, it can be helpful to do the activity for a prolonged period of time (e.g., holding hands for twenty to thirty minutes). If the activity is short in duration, you might try doing it over and over again for a set number of times (e.g., repeatedly saying "I love you").

The idea is to stick with the activity and repeat it over time until you begin to feel more comfortable with that intimacy activity. Since these exposures will involve other people, it'll be important to establish safety by choosing a person(s) you feel safe and comfortable with, having a conversation with them about your intimacy goals, making sure they have consented to engage in the intimacy activities with you, and discussing how they can be most supportive to you during the intimacy activity.

Getting comfortable with intimacy is a process that takes time. Have patience with yourself; go at a slow, steady pace; and consider seeking support and guidance from a mental health professional.

Establish Healthy Views of Sex

Yes, you can (re)establish healthy sex narratives and practices. When sex has been forced on you and/or connected with abuse, it can influence your perspectives about sex as well as your sex practices. Some harmful or unhealthy sexual practices that can result from abuse are: having sex when you don't want to; choosing partners who sexually abuse or exploit you; compulsively masturbating to pornography in which someone is being degraded; engaging in violent sex; minor–adult sex; prostitution or visiting prostitutes; having sex while half-asleep; only engaging in sex under the influence of alcohol or mind-altering substances; avoiding or withdrawing from sex altogether; faking sexual enjoyment or interest; use of abusive sexual fantasies; engaging in secretive sex; making sexually degrading jokes; engaging in voyeurism or exhibitionism; or demanding sex from unwilling partners.

If you notice sexual behaviors that you engage in represented in the list above, it may be that the behavior(s) developed to try and understand or resolve emotional stress related to the abuse. The behavior(s) could be a way that you avoid negative feelings or memories that arise during sex. Another explanation is that they developed to cope with emotions that were sparked by the abuse you experienced. Understanding the connection between your current narratives and behaviors and your abuse history can lead you on the path to healthy change.

Establishing healthy sex narratives and practices requires first identifying which practices or narratives are harmful and unwanted. Several of the practices mentioned can cause harm by generating feelings of unhappiness, guilt, or shame; creating a barrier to you experiencing sex in a healthy and positive way; perpetuating negative beliefs about sex or you as bad or dirty; and decreasing your sense of worth and sexual self-esteem.

Journal Prompts

Grab your journal. On one page, create three separate columns. Label one column "Thoughts," the second "Emotions," and the third "Behaviors." Now, in the appropriate column, take a moment to write down all the ways your thoughts, emotions, and behaviors about sex have been influenced by the trauma you survived.

After identifying the impact trauma had on your sexual beliefs and behaviors, you'll want to identify ways you can stop or change these behaviors. This step is important, to prevent the harm these behaviors can cause over time. However, everyone knows that change is not easy. Changing or stopping sexual behaviors that resulted from abuse can be especially difficult because, although harmful, the behaviors have likely been effective at keeping you from realizing the full extent of the abuse you experienced. Changing unhelpful or harmful sexual behaviors requires long-term commitment, self-compassion, patience, and, likely, support from a therapist, therapy group, recovery program, or a trustworthy accountability partner.

When changing unhelpful/harmful sexual behaviors, it can be helpful to create new healthy practices as substitutes. For example, instead of having sex when you don't feel like it, you can give yourself permission to say "no." Another example: Instead of avoiding sex altogether, you can commit to taking baby steps toward increased physical intimacy with a safe partner, by experimenting with pleasurable touch and clearly communicating your likes and dislikes. Developing new healthy practices can help you begin to develop a new narrative of sex as good and healthy.

A key ingredient of intimacy is to communicate feelings, ideas, and needs to the people you are in intimate relationships with. As a Black woman, you may have been raised to focus on making other people around you comfortable and prioritize keeping the peace, even if it means silencing yourself. For intimacy to grow, it's important that you acknowledge your feelings, ideas, and needs, and communicate them to others. This can be a scary step to take, but with practice you will begin to see the payoff in your relationships. Relationships can grow richer and more fulfilling when intimacy is regularly tended to and nurtured. In the next chapter, we share self-care strategies that will help support your overall healing, while positioning you to experience deeper intimacy in relationships.

Journal Prompts

1. How has domestic violence influenced your level of intimacy with others?

2. How has domestic violence influenced your level of intimacy with yourself?

3. What would a healthy sexual relationship look like for you? What thoughts, emotions, and actions would be present?

CHAPTER 10

Next Steps: Self-Care and Seeking Support for Survivors

Make room for self-nurturing this season. Ask yourself: what do I want and need today? Answer honestly and reward yourself with actions that match your words.

—Alex Elle

The fact that you have survived what you have is no small feat. Because we are members of two devalued groups (Black and women), every day we must navigate a unique set of circumstances that threaten our very survival: gendered racism, discrimination, systemic barriers, biases, harassment, attempts at sabotage and being discredited in the workplace, negative stereotypes, and the list goes on. On top of all of this, you have faced domestic violence. Each one of these stressors has detrimental mental health effects, and combined they are downright toxic—mentally, spiritually, and physically. Yet despite these constant threats, you have found a way to survive. As Lucille Clifton writes:

> won't you celebrate with me
> what i have shaped into
> a kind of life? i had no model.
> born in babylon
> both nonwhite and woman
> what did i see to be except myself?
> i made it up
> here on this bridge between
> starshine and clay,
> my one hand holding tight
> my other hand; come celebrate
> with me that everyday
> something has tried to kill me
> and has failed.

In this chapter, we'd like to offer you some strategies to help you take your survival to the next level—it's time to go from surviving to thriving! The *Cambridge English Dictionary* defines surviving as "to continue to live or exist, especially after coming close to dying or being destroyed or after being in a difficult or threatening situation." When you're in survival mode, you're simply getting by, going through the motions, and often feeling drained while doing it. For some, surviving might look like getting to the point where you can fall asleep at a decent hour at night or be in the presence of a person who shares the gender of your perpetrator without feeling afraid for your safety.

Thriving takes surviving a step further. When you're thriving, you're fully awake, engaged, and feel empowered in your life. Psychologist Thema Bryant-Davis, PhD describes thriving after trauma as the empowerment to (re)gain your voice, body, power, and sense of self. Dear survivor, this is the life we want for you.

As Black women, we are taught to be strong, wear many hats, and deal with a lot of painful things, all with smiles on our faces. We want you to know: Your shoulders were never meant to bear the weight and burden of domestic violence. You have no obligation to settle for a life of abuse and pain. We also want you to know that it's okay not to be strong all the time. A large part of healing is learning how to be vulnerable. There is strength in your vulnerability.

Also, the absence of depression or PTSD symptoms doesn't mean you have healed from domestic violence. Symptom elimination or reduction is an important step in your healing journey, but it doesn't signify the end of it. Healing is ultimately about reconnecting with yourself, becoming the person you want to be, and engaging with the world around you in a way that is guided by your aspirations and ambitions.

Trauma expert Judith Herman nicely captures the essence of a type of healing that goes above and beyond symptom-reduction in her book *Trauma and Recovery*. See if this description applies to you.

> "Having come to terms with the traumatic past, the survivor faces the task of creating a future. She has mourned the old self that the trauma destroyed; now she must develop a new self. Her relationships have been tested and forever changed by the trauma; now she must develop new relationships. The old beliefs that gave meaning to her life have been challenged; now she must find anew a sustaining faith…. In accomplishing this work, the survivor reclaims her world."

Do you want to reclaim your world? Reclaiming your world requires you to uncover the ways trauma has impacted your life, and to learn how best to take care of yourself so that you can create a life filled with value, meaning, and purpose. The goal is to get to a place where you're in the driver's seat of your life, rather than the trauma constantly dictating your thoughts, actions, and emotions.

Your healing is our primary goal for writing this book. Healing differs from coping in that coping is synonymous with surviving. Coping involves managing and dealing with difficulties. Coping is reactionary, whereas healing is a proactive approach to creating the life you desire after surviving domestic violence.

Finally, coping is also often done in isolation. Our collectivist nature as Black women means that we heal best in community, when we are connected to others. You may have heard the saying "No woman is an island." This is never more true than when it comes to healing from domestic violence. The harm of domestic violence was done in relationship, so healing is best done in relationship. Don't be afraid to ask for help. As you continue your healing journey, we encourage you to identify safe spaces where you can heal in community with other trustworthy women.

Keep in mind that challenges and roadblocks can and will arise on your healing journey. Healing is a process. It will take time, and it won't always be fun or pretty. Healing is not always straightforward. You might find that you make consistent progress for some time, then get to a point in your journey where you feel stuck or stagnant. It's not uncommon for challenges with relationships, addictions, sexual concerns, and changes in religion and spirituality to occur.

You may believe healing should occur according to a certain timeline. We want you to know that there is no set timeframe for how long healing will take. Clichés like "Time heals all wounds" may lead you to believe that you will heal once enough time goes by—but the truth is, healing from domestic violence is intentional; it requires effort. If you're not doing anything to address the root of the hurt, then time is just time. For healing to occur, you must be actively engaged and willing to experience the beautiful mess that the healing process can be.

As a Black woman, you may face some unique challenges to healing from domestic violence. As we have previously described, there is a mandate that Black women be strong, independent, assume multiple roles effortlessly, show no emotion, and place the needs of others before their own. This may lead you to conceal the negative impacts that domestic violence has had on your physical and mental health. Because the ability to endure hardship without breaking down is highly esteemed in our community, you may feel ashamed to admit the impact domestic violence has had. The prospect of your family or community seeing you as weak and incapable may seem intolerable. If you're a religious or spiritual person, you may have been taught that God is all you need to sustain you through the trials of life. Because of this, you may feel some initial resistance to some of the things that can help you heal, such as asking for help, expressing your emotional needs and desires, or exhibiting vulnerability. You may believe suffering in silence will protect you from looking weak. But remaining silent will stunt your healing and damage your physical and mental health over time.

For the remainder of this chapter, we offer practical suggestions for ways you can heal from domestic violence. Some may be new to you, whereas others may be familiar or may even be things you've tried in the past that didn't work for you. For the strategies that are familiar, we encourage you to bring an unguarded heart and read with fresh eyes, open to the new possibilities that come from trying again.

Mental Health Services and Therapy

One of the best ways to heal from domestic violence is to seek therapy. Therapy is the process of meeting with a trained professional who is equipped to help you work through past traumas, offer fresh perspectives on challenges you may be facing, guide you in making healthy behavioral changes, and show you new ways of relating to and coping with trauma-related symptoms and your emotions. The goal of therapy is to help you move closer to living a life that is meaningful and fulfilling. The work of therapy is done collaboratively with your therapist.

Rather than simply giving you advice, your therapist's job is to listen, reflect back what they are hearing, and draw on their expertise to give you appropriate feedback and support you in making changes you identify as important for your life. Therapy can come in various forms.

- Individual therapy involves you meeting one-on-one with a therapist.

- Group therapy, with a group of other individuals with shared experiences or backgrounds, can help you learn new skills, work through challenges, and express your emotions in community. Because domestic violence is so isolating, group therapy can help you regain a sense of belonging and connection to other people who have similar lived experiences.

- Families can go to family therapy, to work through challenges they may be facing in relationship with one another. Family therapy can be particularly helpful for you if you have children who witnessed domestic violence or are impacted by its consequences.

- Couples therapy may be appropriate to help you and a safe, supportive, non-abusive partner work to resolve challenging beliefs, behaviors, feelings, sexual problems, or communication issues.

If you're considering therapy, you may be wondering what type of therapist you should be looking for. Because you will be discussing such intimate and personal aspects of your life, you want to feel comfortable, emotionally safe, and understood in the presence of your therapist. The strength of the relationship you create with your therapist is what will make therapy work for you.

When you're looking for a therapist, you want them to be trauma-informed and culturally sensitive. Trauma-informed therapists understand the impact that experiences like domestic violence can have on your thoughts, feelings, and behaviors. A trauma-informed therapist works with you in a way that is sensitive to your needs as a trauma survivor. Culturally sensitive therapists acknowledge and explore the impact of culture on your experiences as a survivor of domestic violence, taking cultural traditions, experiences, and beliefs into account. Rather than treating every domestic violence survivor the same, culturally sensitive therapists create unique treatment plans that honor your multiple identities, values, and perspectives.

There are several directories you can access to help you find a culturally sensitive, trauma-informed therapist, including the following: Therapy for Black Girls; Inclusive Therapists; the Loveland Foundation; Black Emotional and Mental Health Collective (BEAM); Melanin & Mental Health; the Boris L. Henson Foundation; and the National Queer and Trans Therapists of Color Network.

We would be remiss if we didn't mention that going to therapy can contradict some of the unspoken rules and cultural norms in the Black community—one of which is "Don't tell strangers your business." Growing up, you may have heard this rule expressed as "What goes on in this house, stays in this house." One question we must ask ourselves is: Are the secrets I'm keeping making me sick? If the answer is yes, going to therapy can help. The simple act of speaking your thoughts and feelings out loud or telling your trauma story to a supportive and compassionate therapist can be healing in itself.

Another common barrier to seeking therapy in the Black community is the notion that going to therapy means you're crazy. This is a myth. Going to therapy is a wise decision that benefits you and the people you're connected to. It will require that you unlearn some of these rules, which may have served you in one season of life but are no longer beneficial to your survival and healing.

Therapy can feel awkward at first, and it's normal to feel nervous early on in the process. Remember that everything you say is confidential (except when it is necessary to protect your safety or ensure the welfare of another person). As your relationship with your therapist grows and you begin to notice positive changes in your life, you will likely feel more relaxed and at ease.

Spirituality

Spirituality is a sense of connection to something (often unseen or intangible) that is larger than yourself; this could be a Higher Power, nature, a specific community, or the larger human race. Spirituality also involves a sense of meaning and purpose in life. Engaging in spiritual practices is linked to healthy behaviors and attitudes, greater well-being and life satisfaction, and better physical and mental health. The ways you express or connect to your spirituality are endless. Just to name a few, spiritual practices can include prayer, attending faith gatherings or worship services, walking in nature, gratitude journaling, meditation, yoga, reading spiritual texts, reflecting alone in silence, engaging in community service, appreciating music, and artistic expression.

If you're someone who grew up going to church, you may have heard messages suggesting that spirituality and therapy cannot coexist. These messages may have caused you to believe all your problems would be solved if you just had enough faith. And people in faith communities that you belong to may have told you that all you need to heal from domestic violence is to pray and believe.

We are here to say that spirituality and therapy can be complementary components along your healing journey. Going to therapy doesn't mean you're failing your faith. To help you see just how well therapy and spirituality can work together, you might benefit from connecting with a therapist who respects and creates space for your spiritual beliefs.

The sense of community and connection that can be experienced through engaging in spiritual practices with others can be incredibly healing to you. Because domestic violence often disconnects you from existing relationships, connecting with others in spiritual settings can be an opportunity to create mutually rewarding relationships in which you feel respected, appreciated, seen, and welcomed. As we have discussed previously, the inescapable truth is that we need other people on our healing journey. While a spiritual or faith community may not be a space where you talk specifically about the domestic violence you survived, it can help you regain trust in others, give you practice setting your own boundaries and respecting the boundaries of others, and deepen the level of intimacy you feel in relationships. It can be incredibly healing to be around people who love and accept you, with no strings attached.

Movement and Art

When surviving domestic violence, go-to coping strategies can be ones that disconnect you from your body, to escape feelings of helplessness. Movement is a powerful avenue for reconnecting with yourself. Trauma inherently takes power and choice away from you. Movement practices like dance or yoga can restore a sense of freedom and agency: the capacity to guide your body according to your will. Movement can be a very empowering way to have positive experiences in your body, become aware of bodily sensations, and learn how to feel safe in your body. Dance can also be therapeutic, giving you new ways to express and relate to the emotional and physical impacts trauma had on your body. Movement can also be a safe space for practicing spontaneity, building confidence, and using creative imagination.

Expressive arts like poetry, coloring, drawing, painting, music, photography, and sculpture can also provide an outlet to express feelings and memories when words fall short. Art can help you learn to talk about your trauma, by helping you to build grounding skills. By engaging a different part of your brain, art can help you understand your trauma differently and make meaning of it in an empowering way. Because artistic expression is something external to you, it can be a way to externalize the problem of trauma outside of your body and heal the invisible wounds.

Art can also be nice way to connect with other survivors and share your story, if you desire to do so. For example, you may choose to tell your domestic violence story—how it impacted you, and how you're transforming a negative experience into something positive—through a rap, song, poem, picture, or graphic timeline. By sharing your story, you honor your survival and help other survivors know what is possible for them. Rape crisis centers and veterans' health care centers often showcase art through clothesline projects where survivors decorate T-shirts to express their feelings and create new, empowering narratives around their trauma histories.

Activism and Community Work

As a survivor of domestic violence, your voice has power within your family and community, on social media, and in policy spaces. Engaging in activism can be a powerful way to use your story to create community with other survivors, give another woman the courage and resources to leave an abusive situation, or advocate for laws and policies that protect women from domestic violence. Since activism can place you in public spaces and expose you to other people's opinions and potential scrutiny, it's important that you've done healing work before entering into activism.

Keep in mind that activism happens on small and large platforms. Your activism doesn't need to be statewide or nationwide to have an impact. Activism at the community level can be just as powerful as activism at a federal level. The goal of activism is bringing about change. When you use your voice, you may not always see the impact you're having. Oftentimes, change happens over time, at a slow pace. Activism can be rewarding, but also a large investment of time and energy with very minimal tangible rewards. It's important to take care of yourself, to give you fuel for the long run and avoid burnout or compassion fatigue.

There is no one right way to engage in activism. Activism can include writing letters to newspapers or elected officials, running or contributing to a political campaign, rallying for a cause you believe in, or intentionally patronaging (or boycotting) businesses based on alignment with company values. If you're an artistic person, you can also think of your art as activism. By creatively sharing your emotions and experiences, you're raising awareness and being a catalyst for change. Art as activism is particularly powerful because it combines the power of art to move people emotionally with the strategy of activism, which is required to bring about change. If you're interested in learning more about how you can leverage your creativity to ignite social change, the Center for Artistic Activism provides information, training, and resources that can support you.

Mindfulness and Yoga

As a Black woman who wears many hats, you may be accustomed to multitasking. While the idea of checking multiple items off your to-do list at once sounds enticing, most of us are at our best when we do one thing at a time, fully attending to what's happening from moment to moment—also known as being mindful. When you're mindful, you're fully present and aware of what you're doing and how you're responding to your environment. The opposite of being mindful is being on autopilot—doing things in a disconnected way, where your mind is one place and you've lost touch with your body. On automatic pilot, we act without intention or thinking about what we're doing. We all have autopilot moments in life, especially when we're doing things that we have done many times, like driving to work or cooking a familiar meal. But being constantly on autopilot leaves us vulnerable to worry, anxiety, and acting out of character in stressful situations.

Practicing mindfulness in your daily life positions you to do the work of healing from trauma. When you're mindful, you're better able to cope with triggers, and to distinguish a trauma memory from the actual experience of danger. Mindfulness helps you detach from negative thoughts and shift your attention to more productive thoughts. When we're mindful of what's happening here and now, we're better able to catch early signals of bodily sensations (e.g., pain, tension) or emotions that need our attention. Practicing mindfulness teaches us how to observe our thoughts, rather than becoming controlled by them. Mindfulness also helps us to get information from our senses, rather than relying exclusively on thoughts to guide our emotions and behavior.

When it comes to practicing mindfulness, there are numerous options. You can practice sitting down, walking, standing, lying down, or through movement like yoga or qigong. Experiences of trauma impact the relationship that you have with your body. Connecting through yoga or another movement practice can support your healing in other ways, providing things such as intimacy with yourself and others, and greater insight and awareness into your mind, body, and soul. Mindfulness can also be practiced while doing daily activities like eating, driving, showering, brushing your teeth, combing your hair, or doing chores around the house. The key to merging mindfulness with daily activities is to pay attention to your five senses, to keep you connected to the present moment. During mindfulness practice, pay attention to what you're hearing, smelling, tasting, feeling, and seeing.

Keep in mind, there is no one right way to practice mindfulness, and the goal is not to "quiet your mind." The goal is to pay attention to what is happening as it's happening. As a trauma survivor, avoidance—the opposite of mindfulness—may be a way that you have learned to exist in the world. For many people who are used to operating on autopilot, being mindful is a very new way of being in the world. Be patient with yourself. It's normal for your attention to wander. The simple act of bringing yourself back to the present moment by connecting to your breath or another bodily sensation is being mindful. Another way to ease yourself into practicing mindfulness is to listen to guided meditations. A few of our favorite freely available apps for guided meditations are Liberate, Exhale, Shine, Calm, and Insight Timer.

Take Care of Yourself

Self-care is in the air these days. Everyone from medical professionals to bloggers and social media personalities are prescribing it. Because the term has become so mainstream, you may find yourself wondering what self-care really is. To put it simply, self-care is taking care of yourself—mind, body, and soul. It's about giving yourself what you need so that you have the mental energy and emotional resources to heal from trauma.

There is no one-size-fits-all way to take care of yourself. The key is to check in with your body and spirit from time to time, just like you would check the gas indicator on your car to know when it's in need of fuel. When you sense your tank is running close to empty, you give yourself what you need to feel replenished, rested, and energized.

Your self-care needs can change during different seasons of your life. If you find yourself at a point in your life where you're incredibly busy with caring for children or aging parents, self-care might look like getting adequate sleep, regularly eating nourishing meals, making time to read for pleasure, engaging in daily movement that gets your heart pumping, watching funny pet videos on YouTube, or attending a local social group with other parents or caregivers. The key with self-care is doing things to fill your cup so you have enough energy to do the things you want and need to do.

As you have likely felt the pressure to be a Strong Black Woman, you will need to give yourself permission to take care of yourself. It's not unusual to feel selfish or like you're neglecting your many responsibilities by taking time for yourself. When you find yourself feeling guilty for engaging in self-care, remember: When you're running on empty, you're not much good to anyone. When you take care of yourself, you empower yourself to be the best version of yourself possible for the people you love.

You're Not Alone

As you're concluding your reading, we want to leave you with a few words of encouragement. First, we applaud you for investing time and energy into reading this book. We hope you feel it was time well spent. Most important, we hope you're walking away with tangible tools and empowerment strategies that will support you on your healing journey in the days, weeks, and years to come. We truly believe joy, peace, health, and love are your birthrights. May you never forget how powerful and worthy you are. Feel free to return to this book as a resource whenever you need a reminder or to refresh your skills.

As you approach these final reflective moments, know that you're not alone. You can share the following chapter with friends, family, a non-abusive intimate partner, clergy, mental health professionals, or anyone else in your life who wants to support you. You deserve support, love, and encouragement. Remember that people around you may not always know how to do that, but if their desire is there, perhaps the next chapter can help them.

Journal Prompts

1. What people, communities, or spaces support your healing? If you don't have safe people, communities, or spaces, how could you create them?

2. If you could incorporate one of the practical ways to heal (for example, mental health services and therapy, spirituality, movement, art, activism, community work, yoga, meditation) into your life currently, which would you incorporate? How do you anticipate it supporting your healing?

3. What does self-care mean to you? Which area of self-care most needs your attention: mind, body, or spirit?

CHAPTER 11

For Friends, Family, Non-Abusive Intimate Partners, Clergy, and Mental Health Care Professionals

It's in collectivities that we find reservoirs of hope and optimism.

—Angela Y. Davis

This chapter is written for people who wish to support Black women survivors of domestic violence. Although survivors may also find this chapter helpful for themselves, the language of the chapter speaks directly to supporters. We will focus on common and unique means of supporting survivors, based on each group's role.

Common Means of Support

There are some basic means of support that everyone can engage in when supporting a survivor of domestic violence. Specifically, you can monitor your assumptions, check your understanding of domestic violence, avoid victim blaming, and use supportive listening skills when talking with survivors.

Monitor Your Assumptions

We engage with others based on our understanding of the world, which is informed by our experiences, cultural influences, and messages we have learned over time. Most people believe their understanding is accurate—after all, they have no reason to doubt that until something happens that challenges what they believed. But believing your understanding is accurate can result in assumptions that what you think is also factually true. And it may not be.

In intentional and unintentional ways, we bring our assumptions into our interactions with survivors. So it's important to be mindful of them, which includes awareness of where the assumptions come from—for example, if they are cultural and connected to your identities. Are you unintentionally projecting your assumptions on survivors? Similarly, are your assumptions based on facts or myths about domestic violence? Consider these questions as you begin to check your understanding of domestic violence.

Check Your Understanding of Domestic Violence

To best support a survivor of domestic violence, it's important to understand what domestic violence is, and what it isn't. Domestic violence is purposeful intimidation, assaults, battery, or other abusive acts that abusive partners commit against victimized partners.

Domestic violence is a serious problem, especially for Black women. According to the National Intimate Partner and Sexual Violence Survey, about four out of every ten Black women, and one out of every two multiracial women, experience multiple forms of abuse from their partner during their lifetime (Black et al. 2011). The Center for Disease Control and Prevention (CDC) has also reported that Black women are more vulnerable to domestic violence, and experience it at rates that are higher than White, Hispanic, or Asian women (Niolon et al. 2017).

Despite the name "domestic violence," the relationship is not always violent. While there can be physical violence, there can also be sexual abuse, psychological or emotional abuse, stalking, and financial or economic abuse. Abusive partners use manipulative tactics to exert power, take control, and keep their victimized partner in the abusive relationship. Some of the tactics may include violence, but they can also include threats to keep her fearful of leaving; belittling and demeaning statements, to lower her self-esteem and make her question her reality; isolation from her friends and family who could help to support her in leaving; threatening to take her children so she feels trapped into staying; and limiting her access to finances that might help her gather enough resources to leave the relationship.

As you approach supporting a survivor, it's important to remember that she is working to unlearn a lot of negative societal messages about trust and safety. Don't assume that she feels safe with you just because you see yourself as a safe person. She may struggle with feeling safe with and trusting you. In general, when people experience trauma in a way that makes them feel vulnerable and unsafe, it can take time and effort to build that sense of safety back. In the meantime, they may be vigilant for anything that feels like a threat to their safety. Peer, family, and intimate relationships require vulnerability; as does help-seeking in general. Vulnerability requires trust and a sense of being able to stay safe. Building these are imperative for any supportive relationship.

Avoid Victim Blaming

Many survivors of domestic violence have experienced victim blaming, which can further the guilt and shame they feel and make it hard to want to reach out to others for support. *Victim blaming* is when someone places fault for the abuse on the victim, instead of on the abuser where it belongs. Examples of victim blaming include asking "Why did you provoke them?" or "You knew they were controlling when you agreed to be with them."

As you support a survivor of domestic violence, be mindful of state-ments that excuse the partner's abusive behavior and put responsibility for it on the survivor. This is not always done intentionally; victim blaming can be unintentional and can come from well-meaning people. For example, consider Cierra's conversation with her Aunt Joy.

> *Cierra was in an abusive relationship with her partner, Robert, whom she met at church. Cierra's friends, family, and church members all viewed Robert as an ideal partner because of his strong spiritual beliefs, prominent job, and good family values. Unfortunately, Cierra experienced a different side of Robert that he hid from others. In their relationship, he was manipulative, emotionally abusive, and physically violent toward her. Although it took time, Cierra was eventually able to leave the relationship.*
>
> *Cierra's Aunt Joy could never understand why Cierra would leave such a "good man," as she called him, without trying harder to work things out. She would ask Cierra about the things that happened, and Cierra explained that Robert had a temper and could be abusive in unpredictable ways. She recalled one instance, when she was getting ready to go to work and Robert thought her dress was too tight and too low-cut. He called her derogatory*

names, accused her of wanting sexual attention from coworkers, and shouted that she was unsuccessful in her career because no one could look at her and take her seriously. He did all of this before throwing hot coffee all over her dress and pushing her to the ground in her closet—then insisted that she change clothes. He later surprised her at work to see what she was wearing.

When Cierra explained this example, Aunt Joy replied, "Well, what did the dress look like? Was it one of the short ones you have?" She went on to say, "I don't think he needed to be mean about it, but perhaps you could wear something more appropriate for work." Aunt Joy went on to say that she loved Robert's strong spiritual beliefs and family values, which she believed influenced his expectations of Cierra. Aunt Joy ended the conversation by saying that Cierra should consider limiting her interactions with coworkers, because no man is going to want to question those relationships. Ultimately, Aunt Joy suggested that Cierra learn from this experience so that she could be different in her next relationship.

Questioning Cierra's clothing and implying that Robert was justified in his treatment of Cierra is victim blaming. Saying "I don't think he needed to be mean" is minimizing the hurt and harm that Robert caused in physically and emotionally abusing Cierra. Suggesting that Cierra is the one who needs to be different (e.g., dress differently) in her next relationship is also victim blaming and justifies Robert's response to Cierra's clothing. In this example, you might also notice that Aunt Joy has not checked her own assumptions about what spiritual beliefs look like in relationships, or how Cierra should have conformed to Robert's. Aunt Joy may have intended to help Cierra, but her victim blaming statements had a very different impact.

Use Supportive Listening Skills

It would have been more helpful for Aunt Joy to use supportive listening skills when speaking with Cierra. In fact, everyone supporting a survivor would benefit from learning more about these skills, which help facilitate safety, trust, and understanding.

1. **Be nonjudgmental.** Listen to the survivor's experience without judgment based on your own assumptions and understanding. Be open to her thoughts and feelings being different than how you think she should think or feel. Monitoring your assumptions is a good foundation for being nonjudgmental.

2. **Remind her that it's not her fault.** The survivor may have internalized a sense of victim blaming and may be carrying around self-blame as a result. It's important to remind her that violence and abuse toward her is not her fault. She didn't do anything to deserve it. She can control her own behavior, but she couldn't control how someone else responded to her.

3. **Show respect, compassion, and empathy.** Being harmed by someone you love is unimaginable. It's important to respect the decisions and choices that the survivor had to make along the way. Many of those decisions were made so that she could survive the abusive relationship. Respect the strength and courage it took for her to leave. Have compassion for what she has been through. Respond with empathy as you imagine what it took to survive.

4. **Validate her experience.** Believe the survivor and allow for her experience to be her truth. Use statements such as "I believe you."

5. **Be mindful of your nonverbal language.** Without knowing it, we often communicate with facial expressions and other body language. For example, raised eyebrows indicate surprise, a scrunched face can indicate disdain, and crossed arms can indicate disapproval. Be mindful that your body language speaks just as loudly as your voice.

Supporting as a Friend or Family Member

Being a supportive friend or family member will require all of the common means of support that are listed above. Additionally, your role requires patience and understanding, as you work to address any changes that have occurred in your relationship. Abusive partners often isolate the victimized partner so that they don't have close and supportive people around them. Is that something that you have seen happen with the survivor you're supporting? Perhaps her abusive partner moved her away from you or made her stop spending time with you. These are manipulative tactics abusive partners use to remove people who may speak the truth about what they see in the relationship. It also creates greater reliance on the abusive partner as the only (or major) means of support for the survivor.

As you work to rebuild or strengthen your relationship, remember: The abuse is the fault of the abusive partner. Your friend or family member is not at fault, and neither are you. Sometimes friends and families can get into a mindset of "I should have known what was happening," or "I should have done something to stop this." Perhaps you feel that you should have gotten her out or helped sooner. These thoughts are natural and understandable. However, they are not helpful. Neither is the guilt or shame that comes with them.

The isolation that abusive partners create is meant to keep supportive people away from the person they are abusing. They also use manipulative tactics such as denial and minimization to make it seem like everything is perfect in the relationship. They will do everything in their power not to let the truth of the violence or abuse come to light. Now that it has come to light, focus your attention on helping your friend or family member move forward. That will require you to let go of the should've, could've, would've thinking.

As you work to strengthen your relationship, you must recognize that your friend or family member has gone through a traumatic experience and may have different needs than they once did. Your patience and support will be important for her process of understanding what she needs. Be open to her change, growth, development, and new approaches. Also, inquire about what she is working on and learning, and how she is growing and changing. Ask her how you can support her in her process, and of course, remember your supportive listening skills during those conversations.

As you inquire about her growth, change, and overall healing journey, be mindful of pushing for information that she may not want to share. This is where your patience is again required. She may want to tell you about the specific instances of violence and abuse that she experienced, and she also may not. Talking about it can be triggering, retraumatizing, or just plain difficult. Imagine anything in your life that you have experienced where you felt a great deal of fear, worry, shame, confusion, or anger. You may not have wanted to share every detail of the situation that led to those feelings. You would have shared what you wanted, and you had the right to do so. So does she.

Allow for her to go at her own pace, and be mindful of talking it personally and making her feel guilty. She likely lost a lot of power and control within her abusive relationship. Letting her take control of this process, with you in a supportive role that follows her lead, allows for her to have power and take control over her experience.

Supporting as a Non-Abusive Intimate Partner

Much of the friends and family section might apply to you, as a non-abusing intimate partner. Before you move on, here, please review the sections above. As discussed in the friends and family section, your patience toward your partner is imperative, as she will need to build safety and trust.

Safety and trust are a foundation for any healthy relationship. But developing safety and trust takes time, even without a history of domestic violence for one (or both) partners. With a domestic violence history, developing safety and trust can take more time and require even more effort.

Most relationships start off going well, which is why people agree to be in them. Partners express interest in each other, they are typically the best versions of themselves, and they are considerate and thoughtful of the other person. But in abusive relationships, there is a chance that the abusive partner is no longer the best version of themselves. In fact, they may turn into the worst version. They are not considerate, thoughtful, or even kind to the partner they are abusing. Instead, they are manipulative, hurtful, and dangerous. Safety and trust are shattered in a relationship with someone like that. And they're shattered not only with that relationship—the issues of not being safe and able to trust someone can become generalized to other relationships, including yours.

Safety and trust are important parts of intimacy within your romantic relationship. As you approach intimacy (whether the intimacy is emotional, physical, spiritual, or something else) with your partner, ask her what she needs, and be patient if she doesn't know or if it changes. In fact, each time you enter an intimate moment, especially physical intimacy, ask her how she feels, what she needs, and if your intimacy is okay. Is intimacy desired? Abusive partners exert power and control over their partners in a way that takes away their choices and leaves them at the will of the abusive partner. Building safety and trust around intimate moments requires both partners to feel a sense of control over what is happening. Allow for your partner to know she is in control of herself. In doing so, it will be important to avoid language that is pressuring, such as ultimatums, or other things that are controlling, such as bartering for what you want.

Many dynamics in the relationship can be triggering to your partner. Being triggered means something occurs to remind you of something in the past, and brings you back to how you felt then. People can be triggered by other people, places, things, events, words, conversations, smells, touch, and more. It happens without thought or intention. Your partner is not trying to be triggered, and most likely, she doesn't want to be triggered. However, something may come up that reminds her of her past abusive relationship, and for a moment (or for a while) she may experience thoughts (e.g., *I'm not safe*) or feelings (e.g., being scared) that she had in the past situation. For example, she can feel triggered by physical intimacy in your relationship, especially if there was sexual violence and abuse in her abusive relationship. She may feel triggered by verbal arguments that you have, even if they are normal for relationships, especially if fighting was present in her abusive relationship. She could be triggered if you request that she spend more time with you and less time with her friends or family, especially if she was isolated in her abusive relationship.

There are a few things you can do if your partner feels triggered. You can allow her to take the space she needs to process what she is feeling. You might say to her, "I want to give you your space to process what you need right now." You might also let her know that you can be there with her while she processes it, or you can process with her when she is ready. Again, it's important for you to be patient and to allow her to have power and control over what she needs.

Being patient is another part of allowing her to have space when she is triggered. Instead of telling her to snap out of it, move on, or get over it, you can tell her to take the time she needs. You can use your supportive listening skills to be nonjudgmental; remind her that it's not her fault; show respect, compassion, and empathy for her; validate her experience; be mindful of your nonverbal language; and ask for clarity on things you don't understand.

We can't always predict what will trigger someone; they can't always predict it either. Although your partner may be working to understand and anticipate her triggers, there are likely to be some that are unexpected. It can also be hard to communicate while someone is triggered, or soon after. The moment of being triggered is filled with emotions that make communication challenging, such as fear, worry, anxiety, sadness, confusion, etc.

You can preemptively work on communication in your relationship, so that both of you can better express how you feel, when she is triggered. Specifically, see if you can work on the expression of your thoughts and feelings with each other. Practice listening to each other. When you listen, ask each other what you need. Respond by expressing your understanding of what you heard, and check to see if your understanding is correct.

As you communicate, be open to your partner expressing that she experienced something, even if you didn't intend for her to experience it (or experience it in that way). In other words, there is a difference between what you intend to do and the impact of how she experiences it. Validate her experience as truthful for her. Be open to understanding that her trigger is about her abuse, and although you're involved in what is triggering to her, the thoughts and feelings that resurface are not about you, personally. To the best extent that you can, avoid taking it personally.

Finally, it's important for you to be patient with yourself during this time. You won't have all the right answers, and you may make mistakes. However, remember that you're trying. You reading this book is one piece of evidence for that. Also, you're not her only support. She may have been isolated once before. Let your relationship be one that encourages her to use her other support systems, such as her friends and family, clergy members, or mental health professionals.

Supporting as a Clergy Member

In addition to what we discussed in the Common Means of Support section, there are some specific ways that you can support a survivor as a clergy member. It makes sense that a survivor of domestic violence would seek support from a person within their faith. Religion and spirituality are often thought of when it comes to healing, as are the leaders of religious and spiritual practices. One's personal faith can also instill hope and peace, and allow for the healing that's needed following a trauma. This is often true for many Black women, who use faith to get through some of the most challenging times of life.

Although religion and spirituality can be helpful to the healing process for a survivor, they can also be difficult, because of anti-divorce messages that have existed, scriptures that reflect domestic violence and sexual assault, and gender-role stereotypes within teachings. Consider survivor Beverly Gooden's message: "I stayed because my pastor told me that God hated divorce. It didn't cross my mind that God might hate abuse, too."

This is an example of how religious and spiritual teachings can influence how the survivor responds to the relationship that she is in. In addition to long-standing religious beliefs about marriage and divorce, a survivor might hold religious beliefs about being submissive to the male partner in a relationship. These messages can create a hierarchical relationship where she may feel stuck, without a voice, and without choice of leaving the relationship. As a Black woman, she may already be faced with cultural messages of taking care of her family at all costs and putting everyone else's needs before her own. She may then view her relationship as one she cannot leave. She may worry about how you, as a clergy member, view her and her experiences.

As clergy, provide space where the survivor can speak about her experiences, without judgment or fear of spiritual consequences. As you read in the Common Means of Support section, check your assumptions about her experiences, which requires that you consider the cultural influences for those assumptions. For example, how does your identity as clergy influence how you understand violence and abuse in relationships? How does it influence your understanding of if, why, or when a relationship should end? How does it influence your understanding of relationship dynamics and expectations, overall? Consider these questions for a moment.

Providing a space where a survivor can speak about her experience requires more than a one-on-one space with you. It also requires that you create an overall environment within the faith-based community that is welcoming of survivors and open to supporting them through their experience. To achieve this, you might consider your teachings.

- Do your messages convey openness to people making decisions that are best for them and their safety, or are they rooted in teachings that have historically told women to quietly follow their male partner and work through any issues in the relationship?

- Do your messages convey openness to same-sex partnerships, or are they rooted in teachings that have historically silenced women who are in relationships with women? Women can abuse women; is there space in your faith-based community and teachings for that understanding?

- Consider how a survivor will feel coming forward to ask you for help, or to ask for help from others in your faith-based spaces. Will they be validated? Will they be welcomed? Your teachings can undergird these messages and are one way to support survivors before they even come forward.

Once a survivor *has* come forward, it's critically important to encourage their continued participation in the faith community. Remember that abusive partners often isolate the partner they are victimizing, so that she doesn't have support and encouragement to leave the relationship. The survivor may have been isolated from your faith community. She may need support in rebuilding connections because of that isolation. She may also feel worried about the judgment and perception of others, specific to faith-based messages.

Keep in mind that the survivor may also be judging herself. In addition to self-judgment about being in an abusive relationship, the survivor may have internalized the messages that tell her she should stay, follow her partner, and make the relationship work. Ensure that she knows she is welcome in the faith community, support her engagement, and ensure that others continue to engage with her in a nonjudgmental way.

The survivor may also be judging herself around her relationship with her Higher Power. For example, when people are in challenging or tumultuous situations, they often ask God why the situation is occurring or why it's happening to them, specifically. The survivor you're supporting may question where God was in her relationship, and in her life at that time. There may have been a period where the spiritual strength that was needed to leave the relationship was weakened. Perhaps she's still recovering from this spiritual weakening and she needs your support and guidance in that area. Or perhaps her faith was the strength that got her through the abusive relationship. You can also support and encourage that conversation. Assess where she is with her faith and ask her where she would like to be.

It's important to have patience with the process of building safety and trust in your relationship with a survivor. As you support the survivor of domestic violence, remember to validate her experiences, support her strength in leaving a harmful situation, and remind her that it was not her fault.

Supporting as a Mental Health Care Professional

As you likely know, it can be hard for Black women to seek professional help. There are many cultural messages that stigmatize those seeking mental health services. For many of the same reasons, it can be especially hard for Black women to seek services to address the trauma of domestic violence. Reviewing chapters 1 and 2 of this book can help lay the foundation about the challenges for Black women in domestic violence relationships. Such a foundation would be imperative to your work supporting a survivor.

In addition to what we discussed in the Common Means of Support section, there are some specific ways you can support a survivor as a mental health care professional. Before you begin working with a survivor, it's ethically imperative that you understand the limits of your training and competence to work with trauma survivors—and survivors of domestic violence, specifically. You may have a strong desire to help, but appropriate training and education are needed for you to be most helpful. Consider continuing education opportunities that can increase your learning, and consultation with colleagues who can support your work. Although you need to understand the survivor's personal experience, and may ask her to share, it's not her responsibility to educate you about the pain and trauma of domestic violence.

As in all therapeutic relationships, establishing a sense of safety and trust is imperative for the process of therapy to be successful. This is especially true for a trauma survivor, whose general sense of safety and trust may have been disrupted by the violence and abuse she experienced. Show patience and understanding within the therapy process. Approach her behavior within the context of what she has experienced. That will require taking a strengths-based approach to your understanding of her. If she is defensive in a session, consider how the defensiveness could be helping her. Perhaps it's self-protective and making her feel safe. Perhaps it's an indicator that she is struggling with trust in the therapy relationship. Even when the behaviors are unhelpful in the long term, consider how they may help her in the moment. Apply this type of strengths-based approach to any challenges that arise in therapy.

Another part of building trust in the relationship with a survivor is being consistent and sharing your power. Building trust almost always requires that people do the things that they say they will do, including being available when they say they will be available. In that regard, be consistent, reliable, and present for her appointments. When you need to reschedule, do so as far in advance as possible, make every effort to reschedule and not allow for significant time gaps between appointments, and be transparent (to the extent it's appropriate) about why you need to cancel. These steps help the survivor see that you're present for her and that she can count on you.

There is an obvious hierarchy within the therapeutic relationship structure. A survivor of domestic violence has left a relationship where there was also a hierarchy, and she was at the bottom of it. In working with a survivor, not only is it important to understand her relationship dynamics in that way, but it's also important to talk about your therapeutic relationship dynamics in the same way. That requires that you understand and acknowledge the power that you have within the relationship. What you do and say matters even more because of that position of power. Consider if there are also ways that you can share power with the survivor. Power and control have been taken from her in her abusive relationship; how might you support her in getting it back? Take a moment to think about the ways that you have learned to share power with clients in general. Then, think about the methods that might be especially helpful for a survivor of domestic violence.

One way of sharing power is allowing for the survivor to help guide the content of your sessions. Although you may have an agenda for the flow of the session, and the content that needs to be covered, allow for your agenda to be tentative and flexible to her needs. Allow the process of covering the content to be as fast or slow as she requires. For example, be mindful of pushing her to disclose details of her abuse early on or in too much detail. The intake session can be a common place to inquire about abuse history. Inquiring is important to the therapeutic process, but be okay with her sharing much or little detail, and potentially needing to return to that topic in later sessions. Let her make decisions about sharing her experience for herself.

In the process of supporting a survivor, be mindful that she may become triggered, and have appropriate support in place. As she speaks about her trauma, she may reexperience the memories, thoughts, and emotions that she had at the time of the trauma. She may be retraumatized. This is where your trauma training is essential. Talking about the trauma is hard and some people may feel worse in the moment (and for some time after), but that doesn't mean the trauma conversation should be avoided. Instead, it should be done in collaboration with the survivor, who sets the pace for it. It should also be done after you have reviewed coping strategies with the survivor, such as meditation, mindfulness, or grounding exercises. You can also encourage her to make a list of supportive people that she can turn to when she leaves the therapy room but is still triggered by the conversation. When you and she review her trauma, ensure that you have a safety plan, in case she becomes significantly dysregulated.

In the moments before, during, and after trauma discussions, ensure that you assess her current safety. This may be about physical safety from the abusive partner. Is she completely out of the relationship? Is the abusive partner still trying to contact her? Are they stalking her? These are questions to think about, given that leaving an abusive relationship is a process that is not always over when the survivor has declared it is. Throughout therapy, continue to assess the survivor's actual and perceived physical safety. Also assess for emotional safety. To that end, specifically ask her if she is having, or has had, thoughts of harming herself or of suicide. Assessing this is connected to physical and emotional safety.

As you're assessing the survivor's experience, be mindful of comorbid diagnoses. The survivor may or may not have post-traumatic stress disorder or other trauma-related disorders. It's well known that trauma can lead to many other diagnoses, such as depression, anxiety, substance use as a means of coping and avoiding, and panic disorders. Despite the official diagnoses that you arrive at, it will be important to take a trauma-informed approach to understanding and treating her symptoms.

Lastly, be mindful of the time that it takes to heal. Some settings, or therapeutic orientations, may require short-term treatment. Addressing the pain and trauma of domestic violence is a marathon, not a sprint. As best you can, allow for treatment to last as long as the survivor needs it. If you assess that the survivor may need longer-term therapy than you can offer, be transparent in that conversation with her and provide an appropriate referral to another provider who may be able to assist her. Again, share power by allowing her to be a part of that decision-making process.

A Moment to Pause and Reflect

You read this chapter because you want to support a survivor of domestic violence. There was a lot of information here about how you can support, based on your relationship to the survivor, and how people can support in general. As you conclude this chapter, take a moment to reflect on what you have learned. What is the central message that you're taking away? Also, consider your general thoughts and feelings right now. Grab a notebook and something to write with and write down your reflections after reading this information. When you have finished your general reflections, answer the questions below.

Journal Prompts

1. What information was most helpful within the Common Means of Support section?

2. What information was most helpful within a section that was not written specifically for your group?

3. Overall, how will your approach to a survivor be informed by what you have read here?

4. What information will you share with someone else who also wants to support a survivor?

References

Abrams, J. A., A. Hill, and M. Maxwell. 2019. "Underneath the Mask of the Strong Black Woman Schema: Disentangling Influences of Strength and Self-Silencing on Depressive Symptoms Among U.S. Black Women." *Sex Roles* 80: 517-526. https://doi.org/10.1007/s11199-018-0956-y.

Abrams, J. A., M. Maxwell, M. Pope, and F. Z. Belgrave. 2014. "Carrying the World with the Grace of a Lady and the Grit of a Warrior: Deepening Our Understanding of the 'Strong Black Woman' Schema." *Psychology of Women Quarterly* 38 (4): 503-518. https://doi.org/10.1177/0361684314541418.

Akinsulure-Smith, A. M., T. Chu, E. Keatley, and A. Rasmussen. 2013. "Intimate Partner Violence Among West African Immigrants." *Journal of Aggression, Maltreatment and Trauma* 22 (2): 109-126.

American Psychiatric Association. 2013. *Diagnostic and Statistical Manual of Mental Disorders (DSM-5)*. Washington, DC: American Psychiatric Association Publishing.

Badenes-Ribera, L., D. Frias-Navarro, A. Bonilla-Campos, G. Pons-Salvador, and H. Monterde-i-Bort. 2015. "Intimate Partner Violence in Self-Identified Lesbians: A Meta-Analysis of Its Prevalence." *Sexuality Research and Social Policy* 12 (1): 47-59.

Balsam, K. F., and D. M. Szymanski. 2005. "Relationship Quality and Domestic Violence in Women's Same-Sex Relationships: The Role of Minority Stress." *Psychology of Women Quarterly* 29 (3): 258-269.

Beck, A. T. 2002. "Cognitive Models of Depression." In R. L. Leahy and E.T. Dowd (eds.) *Clinical Advances in Cognitive Psychotherapy: Theory and Application*: 29-61. New York: Springer Publishing Company.

Bernstein, B. 2019. "Empowerment-Focused Dance/Movement Therapy for Trauma Recovery." *American Journal of Dance Therapy* 41 (2): 193-213.

Black, M. C., K. C. Basile, M. J. Breiding, S. G. Smith, M. L. Walters, M. T. Merrick, J. Chen, and M. R. Stevens. 2011. "The National Intimate Partner and Sexual Violence Survey (NISVS): 2010 Summary Report." Atlanta, GA: National Center for Injury Prevention and Control, Centers for Disease Control and Prevention.

Bows, H. 2020. "Preventing Sexual Violence Against Older Women." In *Preventing Sexual Violence: Problems and Possibilities*, edited by Stephanie Kewley and Charlotte Barlow. Bristol, England: Bristol University Press.

Brown, B. 2012. *Daring Greatly: How the Courage to Be Vulnerable Transforms the Way We Live, Love, Parent, and Lead.* New York: Avery.

Brown, B. 2018. "Supersoul Sessions: The Anatomy of Trust." Retrieved from https://brenebrown.com/videos/anatomy-trust-video.

Bryant-Davis, T. [@dr.thema]. (2021, January 21). *Quiet the opinions, expectations, pressures, demands, insecurities so you can hear your heartbeat. Then you will know…#clarity #perspective #innerpeace* [Photograph]. Instagram. Retrieved from https://www.instagram.com/p/CKT7ZOUlQcf/?utm_medium=copy_link

Bryant-Davis, T. 2005. *Thriving in the Wake of Trauma: A Multicultural Guide (No. 49).* Westport, CT: Greenwood Publishing Group.

Bryant-Davis, T., and C. Ocampo. 2005. "The Trauma of Racism: Implications for Counseling, Research, and Education." *The Counseling Psychologist* 33 (4): 574-578.

Bryant-Davis, T., and E. C. Wong. 2013. "Faith to Move Mountains: Religious Coping, Spirituality, and Interpersonal Trauma Recovery." *American Psychologist* 68 (8): 675-684.

Bryant-Davis, T., S. E. Ullman, Y. Tsong, and R. Gobin. 2011. "Surviving the Storm: The Role of Social Support and Religious Coping in Sexual Assault Recovery of African American Women." *Violence Against Women* 17 (12): 1601-1618.

Bryant-Davis, T., and S. J. Moore-Lobban. 2019. "A Foundation for Multicultural Feminist Therapy with Adolescent Girls of Color." In *Multicultural Feminist Therapy: Helping Adolescent Girls of Color to Thrive*, edited by T. Bryant-Davis. Washington, DC: American Psychological Association.

Byrd, D., and S. R. Shavers. 2013. "African American Women and Self-Esteem: The Various Sources." *Race, Gender and Class* 20 (1–2): 244-265.

Callahan, M. R., R. M. Tolman, and D. G. Saunders. 2003. "Adolescent Dating Violence Victimization and Psychological Well-Being." *Journal of Adolescent Research* 18 (6): 664-681.

Cimino, A. N., G. Yi, M. Patch, Y. Alter, J. C. Campbell, K. K. Gundersen, and J. K. Stockman. 2019. "The Effect of Intimate Partner Violence and Probable Traumatic Brain Injury on Mental Health Outcomes for

Black Women." *Journal of Aggression, Maltreatment and Trauma* 28 (6): 714-731.

Collins, P. H. 2002. *Black Feminist Thought: Knowledge, Consciousness, and the Politics of Empowerment*. UK: Routledge.

Dankulincova Veselska, Z., I. Jirasek, P. Veselsky, M. Jiraskova, I. Plevova, P. Tavel, and A. Madarasova Geckova. 2018. "Spirituality but Not Religiosity Is Associated with Better Health and Higher Life Satisfaction Among Adolescents." *International Journal of Environmental Research and Public Health* 15 (12): 2781.

DeFrancisco, V. L., and A. Chatham-Carpenter. 2000. "Self in Community: African American Women's Views of Self-Esteem." *Howard Journal of Communications* 11 (2): 73-92.

D'Inverno, A. S., S. G. Smith, X. Zhang, J. Chen. 2019. "The Impact of Intimate Partner Violence: A 2015 NISVS Research-in Brief." Atlanta, GA: National Center for Injury Prevention and Control, Centers for Disease Control and Prevention.

Domestic Abuse Intervention Programs (DAIP, 2017). *Power and Control Wheel*. Retrieved from https://www.theduluthmodel.org/wp-content/uploads/2017/03/PowerandControl.pdf.

Donovan, R. A., and L. M. West. 2015. "Stress and Mental Health: Moderating Role of the Strong Black Woman Stereotype." *Journal of Black Psychology* 41 (4): 384-396. https://doi.org/10.1177/00957 98417732414.

Ebor, M., M. D. Jennings, and T. C. Thomas. 2020. "RoyalTea: Hot Tips to Sip for Sexual Empowerment" by Upspoken. Retrieved from https://upspokenroyaltea.com/wp-content/uploads/2020/01/ALL-Sips _FiNAL.pdf.

Educational Video Group (Producer). (n.d.). *Malcolm X: "Who Taught You to Hate?" speech excerpt* [Video file]. Retrieved from American History in Video database https://search.alexanderstreet.com/view/work /bibliographic_entity%7Cvideo_work%7C2785586

Elle, A. [@alex_elle]. (2021, October 3). *"This is my favorite time of the year! Nt only is the weather amazing, the visible signs of shedding in* [Photograph]. Instagram. Retrieved from https://www.instagram.com /p/CUlBmoxjB2C/?utm_medium=copy_link

Ellison, C. G., J. A. Trinitapoli, K. L. Anderson, and B. R. Johnson. 2007. "Race/Ethnicity, Religious Involvement, and Domestic Violence." *Violence Against Women* 13 (11): 1094-1112.

English Standard Version Bible. (2001). ESV Online. https://esv.literalword .com/

Everett, J. E., C. J. Hall, and J. Hamilton-Mason. 2010. "Everyday Conflict and Daily Stressors: Coping Responses of Black Women." *Affilia* 25 (1): 30-42. Retrieved from https://doi.org/10.1177/0886109909354983.

Fabian, R., and T. J. Legg. 2019. "Healing Invisible Wounds: Art Therapy and PTSD." Retrieved from https://www.healthline.com/health/art -therapy-for-ptsd.

French, B. H., J. A. Lewis, and H. A. Neville. 2012. "Naming and Reclaiming: An Interdisciplinary Analysis of Black Girls' and Women's Resistance Strategies." *Journal of African American Studies* 17 (1): 1-6. https://doi.org/10.1007/s12111-012-9215-4.

Garcia-Moreno, C., H. A. Jansen, M. Ellsberg, L. Heise, and C. H. Watts. 2006. "Prevalence of Intimate Partner Violence: Findings from the Who Multi-Country Study on Women's Health and Domestic Violence." *The Lancet* 368 (9543): 1260-1269.

Gobin, R. L. 2019. *The Self-Care Prescription: Powerful Solutions to Manage Stress, Reduce Anxiety and Increase Well-Being.* San Antonio, TX: Althea Press.

Gobin, R. L., and J. J. Freyd. 2014. "The Impact of Betrayal Trauma on the Tendency to Trust." *Psychological Trauma: Theory, Research, Practice, and Policy* 6 (5): 505-511.

Gómez, J. M., and J. J. Freyd. 2018. "Psychological Outcomes of Within-Group Sexual Violence: Evidence of Cultural Betrayal." *Journal of Immigrant and Minority Health* 20 (6): 1458-1467.

Gómez, J. M., and R. L. Gobin. 2020. "Black Women and Girls and #Metoo: Rape, Cultural Betrayal, and Healing." *Sex Roles: A Journal of Research* 82: 1-12. doi: 10.1007/s11199-019-01040-0.

Gooden, B. [@Bevtgooden]. (2014, September 8). *I stayed because my pastor told me that God hates divorce. It didn't cross my mind that God might hate abuse* [tweet] Instagram. Retrieved from https://twitter.com/bevtgooden

Gottman, J. M. 2011. *The Science of Trust: Emotional Attunement for Couples.* New York: W.W. Norton and Company.

Gould, E. 2020. "State of Working America Wages 2019: A Story of Slow, Uneven, and Unequal Wage Growth over the Last 40 Years." Economic Policy Institute.

Green, L. 2020. "Negative Racial Stereotypes and Their Effect on Attitudes Toward African-Americans." Retrieved from https://www.ferris.edu /HTMLS/news/jimcrow/links/essays/vcu.htm.

Green Swafford, E. & Stockstill, D. (Writers) & Listo, M. (Director). (2015, February 19). Mama's Here Now (Season 1, Episode 13) [Television series episode]. In S. Rhimes, B. Beers, & B. D'Elia (Executive producers), *How to Get Away with Murder*. ABS Studios.

Harrington, E. F., J. H. Crowther, and J. C. Shipherd. 2010. "Trauma, Binge Eating, and the 'Strong Black Woman.'" *Journal of Consulting and Clinical Psychology* 78 (4): 469-479.

Harris, R. 2009. *ACT Made Simple: A Quick-Start Guide to ACT Basics and Beyond*. Oakland, CA: New Harbinger.

Harris, R. 2008. *The Happiness Trap: How to Stop Struggling and Start Living*. Boston, MA: Trumpeter.

Hays, P. A. 1996. "Addressing the Complexities of Culture and Gender in Counseling." *Journal of Counseling and Development* 74 (4): 332-338.

Herman, J. L. 2015. *Trauma and Recovery: The Aftermath of Violence—from Domestic Abuse to Political Terror*. UK: Hachette UK.

Hester, M., E. Williamson, L. Regan, M. Coulter, K. Chantler, G. Gangoli, and L. Green. 2012. "Exploring the Service and Support Needs of Male, Lesbian, Gay, Bisexual and Transgendered and Black and Other Minority Ethnic Victims of Domestic and Sexual Violence." Bristol: University of Bristol.

Holliday, C. N., E. Miller, M. R. Decker, J. G. Burke, P. I. Documet, S. B. Borrero, and H. L. McCauley. 2018. "Racial Differences in Pregnancy Intention, Reproductive Coercion, and Partner Violence Among Family Planning Clients: A Qualitative Exploration." *Women's Health Issues* 28 (3): 205-211.

Holmes, J. G., and J. K. Rempel. 1989. "Trust in Close Relationships." *Close Relationships* 10: 315-359.

Hooks, B. 2018. *All About Love: New Visions*. New York: William Morrow.

Jones, M. K., K. J. Harris, and A. A. Reynolds. 2020. "In Their Own Words: The Meaning of the Strong Black Woman Schema Among Black US College Women." *Sex Roles*: 1-13.

Kann, L., S. Kinchen, S. Shanklin, K. Flint, J. Hawkins, W. Harris, et al. 2014. "Youth Risk Behavior Surveillance, Unites States 2013." *Center for Disease Control and Prevention Morbidity and Mortality Weekly Report, Surveillance Summaries* 63 (4): 1-170. https://www.cdc.gov/mmwr/pdf/ss/ss6304.pdf.

Kucharska, J. 2017. "Sexual and Non–Sexual Trauma, Depression and Self–Esteem in a Sample of Polish Women. A Cross–Sectional Study." *Clinical Psychology and Psychotherapy* 24 (1): 186-194.

Kuhl, M., and G. Boyraz. 2017. "Mindfulness, General Trust, and Social Support Among Trauma-Exposed College Students." *Journal of Loss and Trauma* 22 (2): 150-162.

Lacey, K. K., C. M. West, N. Matusko, and J. S. Jackson. 2016. "Prevalence and Factors Associated with Severe Physical Intimate Partner Violence Among US Black Women: A Comparison of African American and Caribbean Blacks." *Violence Against Women* 22 (6): 651-670.

Lacey, K. K., R. Parnell, D. M. Mouzon, N. Matusko, D. Head, J. M. Abelson, and J. S. Jackson. 2015. "The Mental Health of US Black Women: The Roles of Social Context and Severe Intimate Partner Violence." *BMJ Open* 5 (10): e008415.

Le Franc, E., M. Samms-Vaughan, I. Hambleton, K. Fox, and D. Brown. 2008. "Interpersonal Violence in Three Caribbean Countries: Barbados, Jamaica, and Trinidad and Tobago." *Revista Panamericana de Salud Pública* 24: 409-421.

Lewicki, R. J., E. C. Tomlinson, and N. Gillespie. 2006. "Models of Interpersonal Trust Development: Theoretical Approaches, Empirical Evidence, and Future Directions." *Journal of Management* 32: 991-1022.

Mackey, R. A., M. A. Diemer, and B. A. O'Brien. 2000. "Psychological Intimacy in the Lasting Relationships of Heterosexual and Same-Gender Couples." *Sex Roles* 43: 201-227. Retrieved from https://doi .org/10.1023/A:1007028930658.

Maltz, W. 2012. *The Sexual Healing Journey: A Guide for Survivors of Sexual Abuse.* New York: William Morrow.

Martin, W. P. (2004). *The best liberal quotes ever: Why the left is right.* Sourcebooks.

Martins, T. V., T. J. Lima, and W. S. Santos. 2020. "Effects of Gendered Racial Microaggressions on the Mental Health of Black Women." *Ciência and Saúde Coletiva* 25: 2793-2802.

Matsakis, A. 1998. *Trust After Trauma: A Guide to Relationships for Survivors and Those Who Love Them.* Oakland, CA: New Harbinger Publications, Inc.

McCarthy, M. 2017. "'What Kind of Abuse Is Him Spitting in My Food?': Reflections on the Similarities Between Disability Hate Crime, So-Called 'Mate' Crime and Domestic Violence Against Women with Intellectual Disabilities." *Disability and Society* 32 (4): 595-600.

McCarthy, M., C. Bates, P. Triantafyllopoulou, S. Hunt, and K. Milne Skillman. 2019. "'Put Bluntly, They Are Targeted by the Worst Creeps Society Has to Offer': Police and Professionals' Views and Actions

Relating to Domestic Violence and Women with Intellectual Disabilities." *Journal of Applied Research in Intellectual Disabilities* 32 (1): 71-81.

Miles, A. L. 2019. "'Strong Black Women': African American Women with Disabilities, Intersecting Identities, and Inequality." *Gender and Society* 33 (1): 41-63.

Moody, M. 2019. "Black and Bold: Lessons on How Black Women Survive Double Jeopardy in the Workplace." *Stanford Social Innovation Review.* Retrieved from https://ssir.org/articles/entry/black_bold.

Mushonga, D. R., S. Rasheem, and D. Anderson. 2021. "And Still I Rise: Resilience Factors Contributing to Posttraumatic Growth in African American Women." *Journal of Black Psychology* 47 (2-3): 151-176.

National Coalition Against Domestic Violence. 2020. "What Is Domestic Violence?" Retrieved from http://ncadv.org/learn-more/what-is-domestic-violence.

National Network to End Domestic Violence. 2020. "About Financial Abuse." Retrieved from https://nnedv.org/content/about-financial-abuse.

Neff, K., and C. Germer. 2018. *The Mindful Self-Compassion Workbook: A Proven Way to Accept Yourself, Build Inner Strength, and Thrive.* New York: Guilford Publications.

Neville, H. A., E. Oh, L. B. Spanierman, M. J. Heppner, and M. Clark. 2004. "General and Culturally Specific Factors Influencing Black and White Rape Survivors' Self-Esteem." *Psychology of Women Quarterly* 28 (1): 83-94.

Nikolajski, C., E. Miller, H. L. McCauley, A. Akers, E. B. Schwarz, L. Freedman, and S. Borrero. 2015. "Race and Reproductive Coercion: A Qualitative Assessment." *Women's Health Issues* 25 (3): 216-223.

Niolon, P. H., A. M. Vivolo-Kantor, N. E. Latzman, L. A. Valle, H. Kuoh, T. Burton, and A. T. Tharp. 2015. "Prevalence of Teen Dating Violence and Co-occurring Risk Factors Among Middle School Youth in High-Risk Urban Communities." *Journal of Adolescent Health* 56 (2): S5-S13.

Niolon, P. H., M. Kearns, J. Dills, K. Rambo, S. Irving, T. Armstead, and L. Gilbert. 2017. "Preventing Intimate Partner Violence Across the Lifespan: A Technical Package of Programs, Policies, and Practices." Atlanta, GA: National Center for Injury Prevention and Control, Centers for Disease Control and Prevention.

OneLove. "Four Things You Should Know About Reproductive Coercion." Retrieved from https://www.joinonelove.org/learn/know-reproductive-coercion.

Patrick, S., and J. Beckenbach. 2009. "Male Perceptions of Intimacy: A Qualitative Study." *The Journal of Men's Studies* 17 (1): 47-56.

Pestka, K., and S. Wendt. 2014. "Belonging: Women Living with Intellectual Disabilities and Experiences of Domestic Violence." *Disability and Society* 29 (7): 1031-1045.

Phillips, B., and D. A. Phillips. 2010. "Learning From Youth Exposed to Domestic Violence: Decentering DV and the Primacy of Gender Stereotypes." *Violence Against Women* 16 (3): 291-312.

Platt, M. G., and J. J. Freyd. 2015. "Betray My Trust, Shame on Me: Shame, Dissociation, Fear, and Betrayal Trauma." *Psychological Trauma: Theory, Research, Practice, and Policy* 7 (4): 398.

Prochaska, J. O., and J. C. Norcross. 2001. "Stages of Change." *Psychotherapy: Theory, Research, Practice, Training* 38 (4): 443-448.

Ramphele, M. (1999). *Across boundaries: The journey of a South African woman leader.* Feminist Press at CUNY.

Resick, P. A., Monson, C. M., & Chard, K. M. (2016). *Cognitive processing therapy for PTSD: A comprehensive manual.* Guilford Publications.

Resick, P. A., Monson, C. M., & Chard, K. M. (2014). *Cognitive processing therapy: Veteran/military version: Therapist and patient materials manual.* Washington, DC: Department of Veterans Affairs.

Rose, T. 2004. *Longing to Tell: Black Women Talk About Sexuality and Intimacy.* New York: Farrar, Straus and Giroux.

Roth, G. 1992. *When Food Is Love: Exploring the Relationship Between Eating and Intimacy.* New York: Penguin.

Search Institute. 2018. "Share Power: Treat Me with Respect and Give Me a Say." Retrieved from https://keepconnected.searchinstitute.org /strengthen-your-family-relationships/share-power.

Smith, S.G., X. Zhang, K. C. Basile, M. T. Merrick, J. Wang, M. Kresnow, and J. Chen. 2018. "The National Intimate Partner and Sexual Violence Survey (NISVS): 2015 Data Brief—Updated Release." Atlanta, GA: National Center for Injury Prevention and Control, Centers for Disease Control and Prevention.

Spates, K., N. M. Evans, B. C. Watts, et al. 2020. "Keeping Ourselves Sane: A Qualitative Exploration of Black Women's Coping Strategies for Gendered Racism." *Sex Roles* 82: 513-524. https://doi.org/10.1007 /s11199-019-01077-1.

Stockman, J. K., H. Hayashi, and J. C. Campbell. 2015. "Intimate Partner Violence and Its Health Impact on Ethnic Minority Women." *Journal of Women's Health* 24 (1): 62-79.

Taft, C. T., T. Bryant-Davis, H. E. Woodward, S. Tillman, and S. E. Torres. 2009. "Intimate Partner Violence Against African American Women: An Examination of the Socio-Cultural Context." *Aggression and Violent Behavior* 14 (1): 50-58.

The American Heritage Dictionary of the English Language. 2000. Fourth ed. Boston: Houghton Mifflin.

The Greater Good Science Center. 2011. "John Gottman: How to Build Trust." Retrieved from https://youtu.be/rgWnadSi91s.

Thomas, A. J., K. M. Witherspoon, and S. L. Speight. 2008. "Gendered Racism, Psychological Distress, and Coping Styles of African American Women." *Cultural Diversity and Ethnic Minority Psychology* 14: 307-314. https://doi.org/10.1037/1099-9809.14.4.307.

Thompson, M. S., and V. M. Keith. 2001. "The Blacker the Berry: Gender, Skin Tone, Self-Esteem, and Self-Efficacy." *Gender and Society* 15 (3): 336-357.

Tillman, S., T. Bryant-Davis, K. Smith, and A. Marks. 2010. "Shattering Silence: Exploring Barriers to Disclosure for African American Sexual Assault Survivors." *Trauma, Violence, and Abuse* 11 (2): 59-70.

Time's Up. 2020. "Black Survivors and Sexual Trauma: Culture, Equity, Safety, Survivors." Retrieved from https://timesupfoundation.org/black -survivors-and-sexual-trauma.

Ting, L. 2010. "Out of Africa: Coping Strategies of African Immigrant Women Survivors of Intimate Partner Violence." *Health Care for Women International* 31 (4): 345-364.

Ullman, S. E., and L. Peter–Hagene. 2014. "Social Reactions to Sexual Assault Disclosure, Coping, Perceived Control, and PTSD Symptoms in Sexual Assault Victims." *Journal of Community Psychology* 42 (4): 495-508.

Waltermaurer, E., C. A. Watson, and L. A. McNutt. 2006. "Black Women's Health: The Effect of Perceived Racism and Intimate Partner Violence." *Violence Against Women* 12 (12): 1214-1222.

Warner, T. D., and R. R. Swisher. 2015. "Adolescent Survival Expectations: Variations by Race, Ethnicity, and Nativity." *Journal of Health and Social Behavior* 56 (4): 478-494.

Watson, N. N., and C. D. Hunter. 2015. "Anxiety and Depression Among African American Women: The Costs of Strength and Negative

Attitudes Toward Psychological Help-Seeking." *Cultural Diversity and Ethnic Minority Psychology* 21 (4): 604-612. https://doi.org/10.1037/cdp0000015.

Watson-Singleton, N. 2017. "Strong Black Woman Schema and Psychological Distress: The Mediating Role of Perceived Emotional Support." *Journal of Black Psychology* 43 (8): 778-788. https://doi.org/10.1177/0095798417732414.

Weatherford, A. (2016, March 18). Tracee Ellis Ross wants to make TV that reflects Black people's real lives. *The Cut.* https://www.thecut.com/2016/03/tracee-ellis-ross-race-blackish-black-girls-rock.html

West, C. M. 1995. "Mammy, Sapphire, and Jezebel: Historical Images of Black Women and Their Implications for Psychotherapy." *Psychotherapy: Theory, Research, Practice, Training* 32 (3): 458-466.

West, C. M. 2012. "Partner Abuse in Ethnic Minority and Gay, Lesbian, Bisexual, and Transgender Populations." *Partner Abuse* 3 (3): 336-357.

Wilson, V., E. Miller, and M. Kassa. 2021. "Racial Representation in Professional Occupations." Economic Policy Institute.

Woods-Giscombé, C. L. 2010. "Superwoman Schema: African American Women's Views on Stress, Strength, and Health." *Qualitative Health Research* 20 (5): 668-683.

World Health Organization. 2005. *WHO Multi-Country: Study on Women's Health and Domestic Violence Against Women Initial Results on Prevalence, Health Outcomes and Women's Responses.* Geneva, Switzerland: World Health Organization.

Wyatt, G. E. 1999. *Stolen Women: Reclaiming Our Sexuality, Taking Back Our Lives.* New York: Wiley.

Shavonne J. Moore-Lobban, PhD, ABPP, is a board-certified, licensed psychologist with clinical and research expertise in understanding and treating trauma, as well as general mental health and well-being, through a cultural context. She has authored articles, book chapters, and numerous presentations and workshops. She also has an upcoming book about understanding child maltreatment in the Black community. She has written and developed curriculum on sexual and interpersonal assaults, and has been called to participate in government efforts to reduce the demand of sexual exploitation. She is an associate professor and training director at The Chicago School of Professional Psychology's Washington DC campus, where she teaches future psychologists to be culturally aware and responsive clinicians and scholars. She is also a clinician who provides individual and community-based services that focus on the mental health and well-being of marginalized populations. Moore-Lobban has contributed to communities locally and nationally as a board member for the Boston Area Rape Crisis Center, and previously for the American Psychological Association's Board for the Advancement of Psychology in the Public Interest, respectively. She is also president-elect of the American Psychological Association's Society of Counseling Psychology.

Robyn L. Gobin, PhD, is a licensed psychologist, consultant, and meditation teacher with clinical and research expertise in interpersonal trauma, the cultural context of trauma recovery, and women's mental health. She is assistant professor in the department of community health at the University of Illinois at Urbana-Champaign, where she conducts externally funded research on interpersonal trauma and teaches aspiring health care professionals how to support mental health in marginalized communities. She has supported the development of mental health professionals by providing national trainings on culturally aware trauma treatment and creating diverse, equitable, and inclusive work environments. In addition to publishing forty research articles on trauma and mental health, Gobin has authored self-help books, including *The Self-Care Prescription*, *The Self-Care Prescription Journal*, and *The Doing My Work Therapy Journal*. Her current professional service includes the American Psychological Association's Society for the Psychological Study of Culture, Ethnicity, and Race, and the Division of Trauma Psychology. She serves on the editorial board of the *Journal of Trauma and Dissociation*, and was guest coeditor for a special issue on discrimination, violence, and healing in marginalized communities. Gobin is active in her community, serving on nonprofit boards and leading workshops centering self-care, mental health, and mindfulness meditation.

Foreword writer **Thema Bryant, PhD**, is a licensed psychologist, ordained minister, and sacred artist who has worked nationally and globally to provide relief and empowerment to marginalized persons. She is a professor at Pepperdine University, and is past president of the Society for the Psychology of Women. Her contributions to psychological research, policy, and practice have been honored by the American Psychological Association (APA); the Institute of Violence, Abuse, and Trauma; and the California Psychological Association. She has served as a mental health media consultant for numerous print, radio, and television media outlets, including but not limited to *HuffPost*, NPR, CBS, Oxygen, CNN, BET, TV One, Lifetime, OWN, and WE TV.

Real change *is* possible

For more than forty-five years, New Harbinger has published proven-effective self-help books and pioneering workbooks to help readers of all ages and backgrounds improve mental health and well-being, and achieve lasting personal growth. In addition, our spirituality books offer profound guidance for deepening awareness and cultivating healing, self-discovery, and fulfillment.

Founded by psychologist Matthew McKay and Patrick Fanning, New Harbinger is proud to be an independent, employee-owned company. Our books reflect our core values of integrity, innovation, commitment, sustainability, compassion, and trust. Written by leaders in the field and recommended by therapists worldwide, New Harbinger books are practical, accessible, and provide real tools for real change.

 **newharbinger**publications

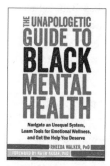
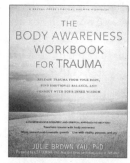
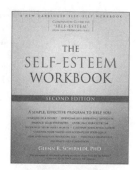

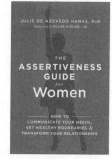

FROM OUR COFOUNDER—

As cofounder of New Harbinger and a clinical psychologist since 1978, I know that emotional problems are best helped with evidence-based therapies. These are the treatments derived from scientific research (randomized controlled trials) that show what works. Whether these treatments are delivered by trained clinicians or found in a self-help book, they are designed to provide you with proven strategies to overcome your problem.

Therapies that aren't evidence-based—whether offered by clinicians or in books—are much less likely to help. In fact, therapies that aren't guided by science may not help you at all. That's why this New Harbinger book is based on scientific evidence that the treatment can relieve emotional pain.

This is important: if this book isn't enough, and you need the help of a skilled therapist, use the following resources to find a clinician trained in the evidence-based protocols appropriate for your problem. And if you need more support—a community that understands what you're going through and can show you ways to cope—resources for that are provided below, as well.

Real help is available for the problems you have been struggling with. The skills you can learn from evidence-based therapies will change your life.

Matthew McKay, PhD
Cofounder, New Harbinger Publications

**If you need a therapist, the following organization
can help you find a therapist trained in cognitive behavioral therapy (CBT).**

The Association for Behavioral & Cognitive Therapies (ABCT) Find-a-Therapist service offers a list of therapists schooled in CBT techniques. Therapists listed are licensed professionals who have met the membership requirements of ABCT and who have chosen to appear in the directory.
Please visit www.abct.org and click on Find a Therapist.

For help, please contact the following:

National Domestic Violence Hotline
Free and confidential
Call 24 hours a day 1-800-799-SAFE (7233) *or* 1-800-787-3224 (TTY)
or Text "START" to 88788
or visit www.thehotline.org (live online chat available)

JUL 2 0 2022